WORLD RIDE

GOING THE EXTRA MILE AGAINST CANCER

Richard Drorbaugh

MasterMedia Limited

Copyright © 1995, Richard Drorbaugh

Published by MasterMedia Limited.

MASTERMEDIA and colophon are trademarks of MasterMedia Limited.

Library of Congress Cataloging-in-Publication Data

Drorbaugh, Richard.

"World Ride—Going The Extra Mile Against Cancer"/Richard Drorbaugh.
p. cm.

ISBN 1-57101-052-1

Designed by Teresa M. Carboni and Jennifer McNamara
Printed in the United States of America
Production services by Graafiset International, Baldwin, N.Y.

10 9 8 7 6 5 4 3 2 1

*There is only one purpose to all of this—
to bicycling around the the world, to writing
this book, to speaking tours, appearances,
consultations and whatever else God may allow
me to do. That purpose is to gain your help in
destroying cancer. I have accomplished nothing
if that purpose isn't realized.*

World Ride Route
June 19, 1993 - May 28, 1994

13,665 Cycled Miles • 32 Countries • 344 Days

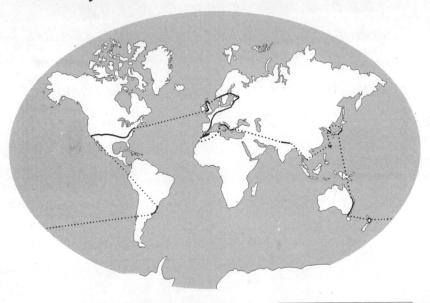

COUNTRIES CYCLED (in chronological order)					KEY	
					——	Bicycled Route
					··········	Other Transportation
USA	Estonia	Spain				
Canada	Latvia	Morocco				
England	Lithuania	Tunisia				
Scotland	Poland	Italy	Hong Kong	Argentina		
Norway	Germany	Greece	S. Korea	Uruguay		
Sweden	Luxembourg	India	Japan	Brazil		
Finland	Belgium	Nepal	Australia	USA		
Russia	France	Bangladesh	New Zealand			

Graphic by Margot Geffen

Contents

ACKNOWLEDGMENTS

Thanks go to Susan Stautberg, my publisher, Melinda Lombard, her marketing assistant, Jennifer McNamara, editor, Antler & Baldwin, Inc., and Tony Colao—the MasterMedia team who brought this book and our World Ride message to you.

The Jaycees World Ride Against Cancer would not have been possible without my fellow Massachusetts Jaycees, the founding sponsor of World Ride. Together we inspired fellow global citizens worldwide to help unite a global community that is committed to ending cancer in our lifetime.

Thanks also goes to: George Gabriel Ash for his strength and encouragement; my girlfriend Nancy O'Sullivan for who you are; Jeffrey Ebert and Peter McIntyre for being the best bicycle teammates anyone could hope for; my three sisters, nephew and the rest of my wonderful Drorbaugh/Hooper/Colt family for all of your love, support and belief in me; fellow Jaycees and Jaycee Senators worldwide; the World Ride Against Cancer Board of Director members Mary Canigiani, Sally Fabens and Nick Baker for their endless pursuit of the World Ride mission; to Billy Starr, founder and director of the Pan-Massachusetts Challenge and Honorary Advisor to the World Ride—without whose help and the help of Louis Shuman and Chris McKeown and the rest of the PMC's dedicated staff, the World Ride would not have reached its full potential; the outstanding staff at Dana-Farber Cancer

Institute for their help with the World Ride event and their passionate work to fight cancer; Alice Tobin and Todd Kurland whose spirited friendship saw me through everything and more; Gary J.H. Wong and Vanessa Galvanek, who drove the Chrysler Neon support vehicle on the cross-country U.S.A. leg and did so much more; and Karen Gross, Diane Barow, Mark Herlihy, Lee Tomlinson and John Shea for their inspiring, focused manner that kept us all on track.

Thanks also goes to the following World Ride sponsors who ensured that 100 percent of all contributions raised went to cancer research: A-Copy, American Automobile Association (Liam Whyte, Dave Juvet, T.J. Andre, John McMann and the Needham office staff), Berkeley Typographers, Bike Nashbar, Boston College Accounting Academy, Boston-Montreal-Boston Bicycle Club, Choate, Hall & Stewart, Chrysler Corporation, Coopers & Lybrand, Copley Systems, Copy Cop, Tony Deluz (illustrator), Doremus & Company, Suzanne Domenici Photography, E.L.I. Computers, Inc., Emerson College, European Restaurant, Globe Corner Bookstore, Harding-Glidden, Harvard Instant Printing, Hightech Signs, Horizon Media, "The Jimmy Fund," Keene Advertising, Lindenmeyr Munroe, MAACO, Massachusetts Volunteer Network Marketing Team, McGregor Travel, Neba Computer, Inc., Northeastern University, the Service Corps of Retired Executives, Shaklee (distributors Dick and Betty Lutts), Sony Corporation, Travelers' Advice and Immunization Center of Massachusetts General Hospital, Video Excellence and Wilmington Publications.

Also, thank you Janet Allen-Wilton, Desmond Alufahi,

Stu Apony, Mike Asbury, George Gabriel Ash's family, Morton Backer, Kevin Bakewell, Sharon Barnes, Hallie Baron, Jim Bashour, Chris Bates, Christopher Beach, Rick Bickford, Jim Bishop, Reverend Boates, Hank Bonney, Jack Bowen, Rick Breer, Matthew Briehl, Pattie Brockwell, Mary Brooks, Jane Brummelkamp, Phil Bundman, Jan Calder, Jim Calder, Lance Chambers, Bob Charland, Joyce Clark, Kitty Clark, Tom Clear, Kathy Collins, Lisa Condit, Phil Conway, Billy Costa, John Cowans, Rick Chrisman, Donna Cusson, Robby Dawkins, Betty DeConto, Paul Desjourdy, Carrie Devine, Faust Ditullio, Maureen Donahue, David Drach, Les Drach, Diana Dunbar, Susie Duvall, Sally Ebel, Travis Ebel, Jeff Ebert's family and friends, Dr. Dean Edell, Joe Eller, Benny Ellerbe, Debby Enblom, Michael Engel, Steve Farrington, Linda Favuzza, Mike Feliciano, Linda Fortior, Sandra Francisque, Susan Frank, Michael Fresolone, James Gagne, Josephine Galvanek, Margot Geffen, Dorothy Girouard, Gary Girouard, Michael Gordon, Lisa Granger, Roy Green, Alan Griffin, Jr., Alan Griffin, Sr., David Habershaw, Alan Hall, Carolyn Hall, Dennis Hanno, Janice Hansen, Jim Harmaty, Judith Healy, Richard Healy, Steve Herrod, Carol Hildreth, Jim Holloway, Connie Holt, Glyn Holton, Jan Hunter, Karen Hurd, Michelle Johnson, Jena Jordahl, Junior Chamber International staff, Joy Juvet, Karen Kalbacher, John Kang, Daryle Karnes, Joe Kasprzak, Ron Kelner, Lindy King, Des Kinne, Larry Klein, Tim Kneeland, Vivian Kreig, Cathy Lane, Scott Lange, Stephen Lawson, Melissa Layne, Gary Lazetera, Laura Limoges, Brian Litteken, Linda Long, Chris Lonngren, Tommy Lupo, Alexander MacDonald, Craig MacFarlane,

Jeff MacInnis, Brad Mader, Chuck Mai, Pam Malumphy, Mel Marcus, Paula Markiewicz, Chris Mason, Dave Mason, Jeff Mason, Joe McDonald, Kathy McDonald, Ellen McDonough, Mike McHale, Mike McHugh, Peter McIntyre's family, Paul McLean, Gale Meehan, Elizabeth Messina, Mark Messina, Holly Metcalf, Brian Moran, Brian Murphy, Robert Murray, Lisa Narva, Cami Newton, Chuck Noll, Mike Noonan, Frank Novak, Kevin O'Sullivan, Tim O'Sullivan, Rosanna Pacitti, Joe Parker, Karen Parsons, Jack Pasquale, Lynn Policano, Tom Portante, Lisa Raskind, Pam Reit, Maureen Ricciuti, Michael Ricciuti, Art Riddlesworth, Holly Riehl, Ken Riehl, Michele Rioux, Malcolm Rosenwald, Pamela Rosser, Elaine Roux, Gary Rubinoff, Al Saboski, Heidi Schiller, Ron Severson, Teju Shah, Lisa Shapiro, Matt Shapiro, Bill Shulman, Matt Siegel, Elayne Forastiere Smith, John Smith, Mark Smith, Roger Smith, Jeff Soloman, Doug Spence, Michael Spiegel, Shelley Spong, John Stamper, Lisa Stone, Karen Strickland, Stubby Stumbaugh, Rick Swayze, Wendy Terry, Mike Thompson, Nancy Thornton, Wally Timmons, John Tirrell, Andrea Tompkins, Gary Tompkins, Peter Toolian, Doug Torosian, John Torosian, Robert Tucker, John Undeland, United States Junior Chamber of Commerce staff, Vicki Wallace, Roy Wallack, Will Ware, Maurice White, Lee Williams, Andrew Wilson, David Wilson, Herb Wilson, Alexzandrina Young, Charles Young, Alicia Zampitella, Debbie Zappen. Thank you for making the World Ride Against Cancer such a tremendous success. I love you all.

FOREWORD

I met Richard in January of 1995 as a fellow recipient of the Ten Outstanding Young Americans Award, given by the U.S. Junior Chamber of Commerce held in Tulsa, Okla. Here was a guy I could really speak to as he stands just about as tall as I do. I was truly struck by his mission and his team's experiences with the World Ride tour—a tremendous feat by any stretch of the imagination.

Having read his book, I found I was drawn into a much more expansive, absorbing, and richer portrait of who Richard Drorbaugh is—a true story about a man discovering a greater version of himself.

The book is definitely about the World Ride tour, but what I found even more rewarding was learning about what all of it meant to him and how he changed because of it. The tour enabled him to experience first-hand differences between people, cultures, environments and lifestyles that took him beyond his present scope of understanding and helped him to see more deeply into who he is, what his connections are with others, and where his life-path lies. For me, there is no more engaging, impactful and insightful book than one that relates a true story of personal growth that I can then incorporate into my own life perspective.

Through this enriching growth experience, he has written a compelling story, being very fair and quite candid in his assessment of the people he met along the road, the countries he traveled through and the dynamics between his fellow cyclists. The trip was very eventful—at times funny, at times very painful and always engrossing.

Richard is an extraordinary young man who has helped the struggle against cancer tremendously. His desire to bring understanding, compassion, and funding to a world-wide forum is heroic. Everyone should have such an advocate to champion their cause and efforts.

ANTHONY ROBBINS,
Author of *Awaken the Giant Within*
and *Unlimited Power*

DEDICATION

To George Gabriel Ash

In the Fall of 1991, the World Ride project was little more than an idea. I was managing and promoting it from a bedroom in my apartment. I had no money, no sponsors and little understanding of the funding needs, organizational requirements and complicated logistics that an international effort of this sort would entail. My first thoughts about it a year or so earlier had been pretty simple: Get plane fares to shuttle between continents and about $16 a day for expenses. I figured I could pack a tent, get on my bike and start wheeling. Nothing to it.

And so it could have been—if the purpose of the ride hadn't been to increase cancer awareness and raise money for research, that is.

As my brain kicked in, it gradually became apparent that if these goals were to be accomplished, every leg of the trip would have to be publicized. Media interviews would have to be arranged, advance publicity planned and carried out, precise destinations set, time-schedules adhered to and so on—all of this demanding an elaborate, round-the-world communications network as well as logistical and organizational talents light-years beyond anything I'd originally envisioned. As I sat at my desk, getting a grip on these new realities and wondering what to do next, over the hill came George Ash, a one-man cavalry.

I'd never heard of George until a mutual friend told me of his public relations background and suggested I call him and introduce myself. This I did, quickly learning that professional expertise wasn't the only thing he might offer to the World Ride project. He offered also the interest and empathy of a man who was in a seven-year remission from cancer!

I hadn't known this before telephoning him, of course, and I was stunned. I'd lost my mother, father and grandmother to cancer, and my sister had recently been diagnosed with pre-cancerous cells. This disease had brought incredible pain and loss to my family, from top to bottom, as surely as if a terrorist had come into the Drorbaugh house, murdering us one by one. It was devastating to me, and over the years my yearning to fight back had grown from impotent youthful anger to an almost obsessive determination to do something. Having no medical or scientific skills, about the only option open to me was to raise money for cancer-fighting efforts and this eventually led to the concept of the World Ride—a Paul Revere mission to the planet warning people of the universal danger of the disease and uniting them in an effort to fund research.

Why not? It made sense. I'd already biked across the United States for the sport of it and been in two or three Pan-Massachusetts Challenges. I'd even entered an event at my sister's home in Texas where I had biked to raise funds for the American Cancer Society. I could handle a worldwide challenge. And the more I thought about it, the more the idea took hold of me, becoming firm, tangible and even attainable. This was something I could really do to battle cancer. And, in time, I settled on it, turning my attention to it with a passion, but unsure of how to proceed and pretty much alone in my enthusiasm.

Now, suddenly, on the other end of the phone, was a man who could not only get this project moving but, as a survivor of cancer, just might share my passion. I was incredulous, not quite sure I had heard George correctly.

"Did you say your cancer's in remission?"

"Oh, yes. Germ T-cell cancer. It was in my lower back. I beat it! I was 17."

"That's great!" I yelled into the phone, bonding with him instantly. "You kicked its butt! Outstanding!"

I could not have been happier for him. Yet at the same time, there was an unsettling mixture of fury in my emotions. He'd been a kid, and he'd licked the disease that had robbed me of my parents and grandmother and which, given our family's genetic links, was likely to take my sister and me as well. I'd never come to terms with this syndrome of devastation and its continuing prospects. There was an unfairness about it that resisted reconciliation, which raised in me feelings of blame toward God and circumstance.

My immediate thought was why George Ash should be a chosen one. Why couldn't this have been my father or mother or grandmother on the phone? Even with the World Ride in front of me, which offered a course of determined action against my feelings of helplessness, the deep sense of bitterness remained, and it showed in my heart as I shot the questions to God.

But it was not fury against George; Lord, no! Above every other emotion at that moment, I revelled in George's victory. He had faced cancer, had defied it—he was victorious! I was elated for him—totally, absolutely, and he knew it—and we hit it off immediately.

Right away he signed on as Chairman of the World Ride Public Relations Committee, making himself available to me at all times, night and day, and he infused the project with purpose and passion equal to mine. Aside from the moral support I so desperately needed, his first-person understanding of cancer and its survivability was of inestimable value. Few, if any, of my other supporters in those earliest days had struggled with the monster, and George's experience and meaningful presentations at our meetings fast-forwarded the rationale for the project, achieving breakthroughs of understanding and enthusiasm where less-spirited and less knowledgable attempts would have failed. I could not have asked for better support in this venture and I blessed the day I had called him.

As the weeks progressed and our friendship grew, and as he brought his vision and persuasion to bear on the World Ride, it occasionally crossed my mind that maybe God, in some small measure, was making up for some of the grief that had been visited on my family. Maybe George was sent to keep me on track ... to keep my dedication at full pitch ... maybe he was sent to help me accomplish exactly what I had set out to achieve—the eradication of cancer within my lifetime. It was true that even in these very early days, George wasn't alone in helping this project. Many talented and dedicated people were now coming aboard and many more were to follow—superb organizers and managers. But George was a special sort of catalyst. His enthusiasm made things happen, and it was easy for me to see him as a helping hand from above.

Such were my thoughts and they continued even after George quietly told me one evening that cancer had returned to him, so sure was I that his remission was a gift that would not be withdrawn.

He down-played it.

"The doctors think it may be any number of things. Cancer's not likely. Don't worry about it," George said.

Several weeks later, cancer was confirmed.

"It's benign," he said. "I'll have to go through some treatment. But, hey! It's benign, not to worry."

He went through surgery, then chemotherapy, then more surgery, more chemotherapy, then a bone-marrow transplant. And I went through hell.

I called and visited him frequently. His spirits never failed. "Now the World Ride has a poster child," he said. When he was almost beyond movement on one of my visits, he started to laugh: "Hey, my mind still works. Let me know how I can help the project. Give me something to do!"

He tacked a World Ride poster to a board at the base of his bed. It was the only subject he wanted to talk about. "When they start the World Ride," he'd tell his visitors, "they're going to wheel me down to the front entrance of this place so I can see the starting line. Fantastic!"

In later months, he was so heavily drugged with pain-killers I could hardly understand him. His face had swollen to twice its normal size. His skin had blackened. On one of these last visits, I came with Peter, one of the two riders who was to accompany me on the World Ride. George's eyes sparkled: "So you want to join Richard in the World Ride! That's terrific! I really appreciate what you're doing to fight this disease!" Then he turned to me, barely able to focus through the pain: "I know you have a meeting coming up with the Dana-Farber Cancer Institute. Now, you let me know exactly when that meeting is scheduled. I really want to participate and give you a hand."

And, again, as he had so often done in these terrible months, he called to me as I was leaving the room and thanked me for letting him be a part of the World Ride.

Not once had I let my sadness for him show in his presence; not once had I cried in front of him or been anything but as casual and lighthearted and as encouraging as I could manage. But not once did I ever leave George's room and walk down the hall without being wracked by sobs and the terror of the thing that was killing him before my eyes.

The end came in early June of 1993, about 18 months since we had first met and two weeks before the official start of the World Ride. He was 25 years old.

At his wake, I knelt beside his open casket and vowed to him that nothing would stop the World Ride. No matter what the obstacles, I swore to him that I would bring the message of his death to the world as an example of someone who died too young and too vibrant, a terrible waste of a good person in a world that needs every good person it can get. George Gabriel Ash would be the World Ride's battle cry to unite a global community against cancer.

And so it was.

And this tribute to him is the matter of first importance in this book.

One

READY OR NOT

Massachusetts: June 19–20

The day dawned sunny and bright in Boston. By 9 a.m. I was wearily pushing my bike toward the World Ride starting line in front of the Dana-Farber Cancer Institute.

Exhausted, flabby, 20 pounds overweight and having trouble even lifting my bike, I had assured the world that I could sprint from the line and ride 14,000 miles around the entire planet. People stared at me, noting my condition and nodding to each other, and I swear I heard bets being placed on my chances of reaching the nearest intersection.

Two other riders had somehow lost their senses and had been mesmerized into joining me on this escapade, and I eyed them narrowly—appalled at the remarkable contrast between them and me.

Our Team—The Right Stuff

Jeffrey Ebert, tanned from the Tucson sun, fit, trim, having just finished some white-water rafting and a 2,200-mile bike trip for the fun of it, pranced around his bike, doing a couple of knee-bends for the crowd.

Peter McIntyre, barrel-chested, rugged, a Captain in the

Canadian Armed Forces and bi-athlete who had once walked across the U.S. for exercise, was just standing around. In his head (I was sure of it) were blissful visions of daunting challenges in roadless third-world countries, his great heart filled with happy prospects of mastering foggy mountains and wheeling along stony footpaths on the edge of 2,000-foot precipices. I half expected him to pull a head of spinach out of his bike bag.

Both men had first heard of the World Ride organization and its round-the-world plan through articles in cycling magazines, and were among the dozen or so readers who forwarded letters expressing an interest in joining me on the ride. From the beginning of my World Ride planning, I had been prepared to bicycle alone, but the Jaycees and other sponsors were concerned about a solo trip of such demanding proportions and had urged me to put a team together. They left the decision up to me and I went along with their suggestion. (The wisdom of their concern was to be amply demonstrated many times in the days to come.)

The Smaller, The Better

In my mind, I had settled on a two- or three-man team rather than chance the problems that might be encountered in the personality mix and dynamics of a larger group, and as I looked through the letters from team-member hopefuls, Jeff and Peter looked better and better.

Both men had extensive cycling experience over long distances—a primary qualification—and in follow-up correspondence and telephone calls, I found them likeable and knowledgeable. Both had a sharp sense of humor, and I sensed that the three of us would probably get along very well.

One very positive aspect was that both of these men could afford to make the World Ride. I would be sponsored on this tour, but other team members would have to pay their own way. They would need a minimum of $10,000 each for the year-long tour—a requirement which had immediately canceled out several other hopefuls. Jeff and Peter affirmed that they had the necessary funds.

Private Motivations

Both also had reasons for joining the team that were compatible with the World Ride's purpose. Peter knew first-hand what cancer could do, having lost a cousin with whom he'd been especially close. He felt strongly committed to the World Ride mission: raising funds for cancer research.

Jeff didn't have a family connection with cancer, but a close friend's mother had been diagnosed with it and her battle touched him deeply.

Another plus was their maturity. Peter was 41 and Jeff was 35 or 36, old enough to have had some sobering experiences in life and to understand the serious nature of the World Ride. Nothing about this project was a lark; hundreds of people were involved, schedules were set, press interviews and meetings would require diplomacy and tact, ingenuity and self-sufficiency on the road would be a must. Considerable inconveniences and dangers were to be anticipated. All of these elements demanded responsibility, dedication and abilities of a high order. I began to wonder whether I'd be able to measure up—whether my younger age of 30 would place me at a disadvantage.

When Jeff and Peter eventually flew to Boston on separate occasions to meet with me and the Massachusetts Jaycees (the founding sponsor) and other World Ride sponsors, there was no question that they qualified for the mission on every level. It was me I was worried about.

Could I, Or Couldn't I?

So, that's where things stood the morning that I straddled my bike at the starting line. Never in my life had I been as overcome with self-doubt and second-thoughts, and the abysmal physical shape I was in certainly didn't help to assuage my sense of uncertainty. After a year-and-a-half of organizing the World Ride, cajoling help from every quarter, promoting, begging, giving talks, hustling for funds and sponsors and sacrificing to the point where I could barely take my girlfriend to the movies or keep my refrigerator stocked—the moment for action had suddenly arrived, and I was afraid of falling off my bike before I got to the suburbs.

All I could think about were the people who were depending on me, confident of the promises I'd made and sure of the convictions I had instilled in them. Jeff and

Peter believed in me. Volunteers and sponsors believed in me. My family believed in me. My reputation, my career, and just about everything else in my life felt as if it was on the same line as my bike. So, sure, I doubted myself, and being up until 2 a.m. that morning working on my bike hadn't helped matters a whole lot.

Things Coming Together

Everything about the World Ride, in fact, had jelled in just the past few weeks—the title sponsorship, the non-profit status and the liability insurance. Even Peter's official military leave to join the team hadn't been pinned down until a few days earlier. We didn't even have our bikes until a day before the World Ride began. Peter and Jeff hadn't even met until 36 hours before we gathered at the starting line. To the best of my knowledge, they had only spoken once or twice on the telephone prior to that meeting. It was like this night and day—incredibly busy right up to the morning of the start. The go or no-go decision always seemed to hang by a last-minute thread.

During all of this eleventh-hour activity, of course, I'd had no time for reflection or to give myself a pep-talk. And over the past year-and-a-half, there had certainly been no opportunity for getting into the disciplined kind of shape required for a round-the-world bike ride. But not until I stumbled to the starting line that June morning, having just finished a thank-you speech to sponsors and volunteers, did I fully realize how poorly prepared I really was. I was ready for R&R on a Hawaiian beach, not a 350-mile bike grind to Montreal starting in six minutes.

A Miracle at The Gate

There was a small crowd of well-wishers mulling around, including friends, volunteers, sponsors, members of my family and my minister (whose prayers I desperately needed), and as I stood there contemplating Jeff and Peter, hoping some of their energy would magically drift my way, a pleasant-looking, middle-aged man walked up to me and extended his hand. He said he was a cancer patient at Dana-Farber and he told me how much he appreciated what I was doing for cancer research. He'd seen the goings-on in the street, asked about it, and then come over to thank me.

As he spoke to me, I can only tell you that a miracle occurred. A bonafide, legitimate, one-of-a-kind, absolute miracle.

From Doubt to Certainty

In the moments I was talking with that man, a total transfusion of spirit took place within me. Every ounce of enthusiasm I had been forced to set aside in the hectic activity of the past few weeks suddenly returned in a tremendous, overwhelming rush. My self-doubts instantly vanished. My mind cleared. I knew why I was there, the solid purpose behind it and the job that needed to be done. It was like being reborn, and I knew in those moments that the World Ride was going to happen and that it would be successful. Absolutely. No question about it. No way was this going to fail. No way would these people be disappointed. Even my tiredness evaporated, and if I hadn't known better, I'd have sworn that even the extra 20 pounds of flab I was carrying had disappeared.

It was that big a change—from doubt to certainty, from second-thoughts to eagerness—all in a matter of seconds.

What can I say? Heaven-sent? I don't know. But I do know that I had no official starter for the World Ride and that, given what had just happened, I didn't need one. Whoever that inspiring gentleman was, he had done the job for me perfectly!

As he melded back into the crowd I made the rounds for last good-byes—vigorously and excitedly— and then jumped on my bike and waved Peter and Jeff to the line.

A second later—while being accompanied by several other bikers who tagged along with us on the early legs of the trip—the first turn of the wheel was made on the 14,000-mile World Ride Against Cancer.

The First Leg

Our first leg was to Hubbardston, Mass., about 50 miles from Boston, and then on to Brattleboro, Vt., for the second leg. You wouldn't think there would be much to report on a two-day, civilized little jaunt like that, but let me log it for you:

Item: The police decided not to clear a path for us through the city. We thought we had this arranged, but they left this interesting job to Gentleman Jim Calder, the driver of our sole support vehicle, who then had to experiment with blocking traffic on Boston bridges, for example, while we scuddled across lanes like a bunch of scared ducklings. (You don't know what scared is until you try to cross-lane one of the Charles River bridges with a bicycle at 10:30 in the morning!)

Item: Peter's bike broke before we cleared Boston.

Item: Some of our accompanying riders got lost—I mean thoroughly lost; we couldn't find them and nobody else could find them—not for hours. Some of them may still be out there.

Item: I ate too much at a rally-stop in Cambridge, stuffing myself in accord with the respected "camel" theory that I could store all this stuff in a hump somewhere for extra energy. I urge you to forget that theory. It gives a bike-rider's stomach the choice to digest or not to digest. Guess which one it does.

Item: On the road between Hubbardston and Brattleboro, in a downpour, Jeff made a wrong turn and biked 27 miles back toward Massachusetts. He'd been traveling at some distance from us so we didn't notice his absence. Needless to say, given the way things go, Jeff didn't have his wallet or any money with him, all of this being in our support van. He managed to rejoin us in Brattleboro after a day of riding and hitchhiking over roads that were akin to Venetian canals.

The Lonely Road

The most important item, for me, at least, occurred on the Brattleboro leg—somewhere in that strange, forbidding, alien landscape of lower Vermont. It was here that I decided to get lonely. My girlfriend, Nancy, was nowhere to be found and neither were my friends and family, and I realized I was all alone and it was going to be that way for the whole time it took to get around this great big world. Oh, I'd have my bike guys with me, but they were practically strangers, and I couldn't really count on them or anything. And maybe, I thought, they weren't as serious about the World Ride as I was, and maybe they'd mess it up somehow.... I went on and on like this for several miles.

It was a bleak outlook, and it got bleaker and bleaker the more I mused about it. (Things like this happen to the mind when you're pedaling endlessly along a highway, counting mile-posts and wondering if your bike would be nice enough to stay upright if you took a nap.) But it goes as quickly as it comes—the outlook, that is. The one thing I did think about clearly was that I was 80 miles from home at that point and if I was already having these hallucinations and feeling lonely, I'd be a world-class case in Nepal.

Although the paranoid musing over my companions came to an abrupt end—I recall a logging truck snapping me back to reality—my thoughts of Nancy rode right along with me for every mile of the World Ride.

Support at Home

Nancy had supported me unconditionally from day-one of this project, patiently putting up with a man thoroughly obsessed with his crusade. I think I was able to make up for it in some measure with the love and attention I showed her, but when the World Ride organization was completed—due in large part to her constant encouragement and business savvy—I immediately jumped on a bike and went off for a year-long ride through 32 exotic countries with two complete strangers. Nancy had known this was coming—that we would be separated—but still she stuck by me and was excited about making plans to hop on planes and meet me in various places.

Any man alive would miss a woman like Nancy. The heaviness I felt after only 80 miles was not a sign that I was cracking up but instead, a verification of my intrinsic humanness and sanity (to say nothing of my unspeakable good fortune).

Such were the events on the first couple of legs, except, of course, for the outcome of Peter's woes (you'll remember that his bike had died in Boston). He had been accompanying us in the support van and Nancy had been her usual supportive self by picking up the needed part for his bike from the Boston dealer with the intention of delivering it to us in Brattleboro. Her car, however, decided it wouldn't go any farther than Hubbardston and she had to call the American Automobile Association and was towed back to Boston. Figuring her options about the part for

Peter's bike, she wisely decided to leave it at the Hubbardston Police Station, which like all police departments, was open all night. Jim (our van driver) drove to Hubbardston at 3 a.m., retrieved the part and delivered it to Peter by dawn.

You see what can happen in just 100 miles or so. Just think, we only had a little less than 14,000 miles to go.

Two

TENDING TO BUSINESS

Vermont: June 21–22

Everywhere throughout the World Ride we were met by individuals, groups and committees connected in some manner with the project—either directly involved or indirectly through cancer research fund-raising or similar efforts. This is what the World Ride was all about, of course, but in the first few days my attention was primarily focused on adapting to bike life on the road, remembering all the things I'd forgotten from earlier rides and essentially settling myself into a physical rhythm that would make the many miles ahead of me as tolerable as possible. Peter and Jeff did the same, but never more than a few days passed—particularly in the early stages of our ride—before unexpected encounters with wonderful, supportive people popped up out of nowhere to remind us of the purpose of our mission.

The Kindness of Strangers

On the way from Hubbardston to Brattleboro—the day Jeff had mistakenly gone on his 27-mile sight-seeing detour—I was surfing along the highway and noticed a couple of people up ahead standing in the middle of the road with bikes. As I pulled up to them, one of them asked if I was the guy riding for cancer. I couldn't imagine he meant me, but he did. They had read an article about the World Ride in a New England cycling magazine, which gave them a general idea of the route and itinerary, and they had decided to meet up with us.

Peter was in the van, wrong-way Jeff was a long way to the south and I was the only member of the team sitting on a bicycle on that road, but it was enough for them and they asked if they could join in on the last lap to Brattleboro—which, of course, pleased me greatly.

Their names were Bruce and Mark. They were members of the Brattleboro Cycling Club and it appeared their main purpose in deliberately exposing themselves to near-drowning in a Vermont rainstorm was to sort of "catch-up" on the news of the World Ride, as they put it, and give the team some support and encouragement. I was grateful to them for refocusing my attention on the mission and bringing home the fact that there were a lot of people out there pulling for us.

I could fill another book with just the names and good deeds of the hundreds of persons who came forth at varying and unexpected times to encourage us and to support the World Ride—somehow always seeming to be there when we needed our spirits lifted.

Martha O'Connor is another example. She was the Chairwoman of the Brattleboro Board of Selectmen and shared responsibility for establishing the Brattleboro World

Ride Day. Besides that, she then paid for four motel rooms for the team! Considering the fact that I was on a strict daily budget of $11.50 (yes, friends, $11.50), you can understand how much the rooms were appreciated. That $11.50 was earmarked to take care of almost every expense apart from airline tickets, ferries and trains. It paid for food, shelter (most of the time we camped out), repairs and administrative expenses. In short, it went for anything and everything. Fortunately, we were to meet a whole lot of helpful Martha O'Connors nearly everywhere we went.

None of the above is intended to detract from the infinite credit due to the Jaycees or the World Ride organization; they were sensationally efficient, and all the pre-arrangements that were made for food and shelter were dependable. But we also relied upon the spontaneous hospitality and generosity of many friendly people along the way and without their help, we probably would have had to quadruple our daily budget. I know I would have, considering my famished condition and craving for carbohydrates at the end of a good day's ride. The only place I could have gotten by on my daily allowance would have been Italy—the mother-lode of high carbos. In Italy, $11.50 could have bought me a five-gallon drum of spaghetti.

Getting Focused

Brattleboro was really the refocusing point for me. I'd come to know my teammates better and I'd broken-in my bike, established my riding rhythm and generally ironed out the kinks and wrapped up the trial-and-error period. Bruce, Mark and Martha O'Connor—and several other supporters and friends of the World Ride who magically appeared here and there—had gotten my attention and served as reminders of the mission's purpose. Settling down to business was now the task at hand, being very much on my mind from that point forward.

This meant that I went to bed at night with the next day's itinerary on my mind. The Jaycees—the term includes the Junior Chamber International, the U.S. Junior Chamber of Commerce, state and local branches and the Junior Chamber Senators (members with many years of outstanding work behind them)—combined to provide the engine for the World Ride.

It was the Jaycees who set up the scheduling and arranged for press conferences, media interviews and meetings with community leaders and interested local organizations. Strict itineraries had been programmed for us, town-by-town, and the Jaycees depended on us to be at the right place at the right time. Their names and reputations were at stake; there wouldn't have been a World Ride without them. I fully intended to do my best to uphold the team's end of the bargain and honor the necessary commitments and schedules.

Now those are the sort of noble and responsible sentiments the world longs to hear from members of my generation, but given the fact that I was way out of shape and also rubbed raw from tail-end to fingertips by uncustomary long-distance biking, fulfilling the goal was infinitely easier said than done.

Great (Scheduling) Expectations

I knew the rawness would pass in time and that my muscle-tone would return after a few more Vermont hills, but on this night in Brattleboro I went to bed faced with a 77-mile ride to Rutland on the following day that had to be accomplished in six hours. Scheduling dictated that the team remain in Brattleboro until 10 a.m. (two radio interviews were scheduled) and our appointment with the mayor of Rutland was at 4 p.m. Not only would the mayor be expecting us, but also on hand would be a covey of media people, so we had to be there. Given the miserable weather and the condition I was in, that schedule seemed a mite tight, to put it mildly. (The Jaycees and Junior Chamber Senators, as I mentioned to the others wryly, were really cooking.)

As expected, at 10 a.m. the next morning it was still raining as hard as the day before when I'd met Bruce and Mark. Head winds (a biker's worst enemy) were vicious, and the only way we could even come close to making Rutland in six hours under such conditions, and in such hilly country, was to shed our 50-pound load of assorted bicycle paniers (mounted bicycle bags) and other gear. We put it all into the support van and headed out on our bikes as light and as unencumbered as possible, praying we didn't have any equipment trouble. We had to pedal like crazy and not pay any attention to rain or wind or to chafed butts and sore legs.

We managed to make it on time, arriving at the party

looking like drenched road-kill. The whole episode was a lesson in raw reality. I knew very well that we'd have many, many more days like this, being scheduled for a morning appointment in one place, then rushing to another appointment in another place a day's ride away. This was going to be the pattern on this World Ride, and while I appreciated the necessity of it, I still kicked myself for not being in shape for it.

I only hoped I'd be in prime form by the time we hit Europe. I didn't even know how to read the road signs over there. (If this had been a leg from Brattleboro, Poland, to Rutland, Poland, we never would have had a prayer of making it on time.)

Another thing that hit home—and this came into focus during the Rutland interviews—was the need to steer the media questions. Peter had had some experience with this when he'd walked across the U.S. and he gave me some useful advice. Reporters tended to ask him questions that revealed every aspect of the walk—except the part that he wanted told—and he had to vector the conversation around so that the right questions would be asked. I started practicing this technique toward the end of the interviews in Rutland so that cancer research and its funding was worked into the lead elements of the reporters' stories. I got better at it as the World Ride continued and it wasn't too long before my interviews accurately represented the purposes and goals of the mission.

Part Angel, Part Administrator

After the meeting with the Rutland mayor and media people, we rode up the road and spent the night at a campground. The next day, our last full day in the States, we had a 15-minute live interview on a local radio station, and then I had to steal away for an hour or so and contact World Ride headquarters and Junior Chamber International headquarters. This was the "administrative" part of my team leadership duties—duties that accompanied me everywhere I went on the World Ride and which you'll hear me moan about frequently.

It had to be done, it ate up a lot of time and it was generally necessary to attend to it either in the morning, when we were impatient to get going, or at night, when I was ready to drop dead into my sleeping bag. On this particular morning, the subjects discussed on the phone included travel plans, overseas airline tickets, publicity, our Canadian scheduling, sponsor updates and a host of team issues—just to name a few. (In these conversations, I always managed to include a "kiss" message for Nancy.)

This was pretty much the way it was to go on the World Ride, day in and day out, a good bit of my energy being expended on everything except riding a bike. I was, after all, the originator and head honcho of the World Ride and every detail and plan was funnelled through me at one point or another. Stuffed into the back of my riding pants was an overnight mail pack filled with administrative papers, and everywhere I went it went. The World Ride was nothing like the cross-U.S. ride I'd made some years earlier or the Pan-Massachusetts Challenges. This one demanded an entirely different discipline!

While I was attending to the administrative stuff that morning, Jeff and Peter went on ahead, in the rain as usual. When I got back on my bike I promptly managed to get lost, losing a half-hour or so before I found my way back to them on the proper route. After a short lunch break (I dined on a hot dog since my budget was low), we traveled on a while longer, eventually ending up in a campground that was half under water.

We had been scheduled for a remote radio interview in Burlington, but the mobile unit didn't find us and I spent the evening medicating my aches and chafes as best I could, trying not to feel too sorry for myself. Cancer victims had a zillion times the aches that I did and I fell asleep with that thought in my head, wholly resolved, in a Winston Churchill way, to see this thing through to the end no matter what. I was also hardening up; I could feel it through the soreness. It was slow, but noticeable, and it cheered me up.

To date, the World Ride had raised about $8,000 for cancer research, a good start. Tomorrow we'd see what we could do in Canada.

Three

BLUE SKIES!

Vermont-Canada: June 23–27

Waking up to a clear, blue sky the next morning has to rank as one of the great events of my life, like my first memory of Christmas. What a treat! The water was still running off the campground like an overflowing dam, and a big Canadian high (good weather) had come in overnight and we knew the leg to Montreal would be a relative joy. As soon as we bounded out of our tents, we stood around with huge grins on our faces.

(FACT: About 80 percent of the days we rode through the U.S., Canada, North Africa and Europe, it rained. That's not a guess—it's a fact carefully noted in my written log of the trip. On eight out of 10 days over the first four months (more than 6,000 miles) we had rain, sometimes light, sometimes heavy, but rain nonetheless. Starting out on the World Ride, we didn't have a clue, of course, that this was to be the case. We were expecting nice days to be the norm and had carefully planned to take advantage of dry, pleasant weather patterns around the world—but how wrong that proved to be! On a bike, rain is cold, penetrating and soaks you. In short, it's miserable, and we were to have 96 days of it out of the first 120 days we biked.)

Scheduling Chaos

The night before our bright Vermont morning, Jim had reached Antoinette (the Montreal World Ride Project Manager) and he informed us that we had a press conference in Montreal at 5:30 p.m. This was in addition to a 9 a.m. newspaper/radio interview already scheduled in St. Albans, Vt., a few miles up the road—what else was new?

As we biked toward St. Albans, almost certain there was no way we could make the Montreal press conference by 5:30, I speculated on how the Jaycees were putting these crazy schedules together. Now, please understand that the whole Boston-to-Montreal route and scheduling had been mostly organized by the Jaycee Senators. In the months ahead, looking back on the World Ride with a lot of experience under our belt, we came to understand just how superbly the Senators had managed that early part of our trip. Very special thanks go to Steve Farrington and his fellow Vermont Junior Chamber Senators for coordinating the interviews and meetings on the Vermont legs and for the tremendous support the World Ride received in that state. But we were still new to this crusade at that stage, concerned mostly with our physical ability to meet the schedule demands, and once again I got to musing about things as I biked to St. Albans that morning. It went something like this:

I figured there had to be two people involved in the scheduling, Person A and Person B. Person A would examine our route, and then pick out the towns along the route that had a newspaper and a radio station and maybe a Jaycee organization. He would then say, "Oh, here's a good place to stop. And there. And, oh, yes, by all means they should stop in East Nowhere, too; I have a grand aunt living there and they can drop by and she'll give them cookies." So, he'd pencil these stops in and then make the arrangements and so on.

In the meantime, Person B, who was mad at Person A and not speaking to him, would be setting up our meeting at the major destination stop for the day. That would be penciled in without the faintest hint of rational coordination between the two schedules, or that any of it could be accomplished by three men on bikes. The only thing these two guys obviously had in common was the shared assumption that we were in souped-up sports cars, able to lay rubber from place to place in New York time.

A Dream Unfolds

While it is true that the scheduling we had to follow was almost invariably a hard race against time, we were also racing against cancer. As we became more accustomed to the media, and more able to direct the resulting publicity, all of us began to realize we were starting to make progress in that more important race. We were taking a little pride in it, and although we often joked about the scheduling, we resented it less. It was a subtle change, but a real one, and I remember thinking about it after we finished up our visit in St. Albans.

Our interviews there had been properly focused on cancer, and the radio interview was especially helpful to the local Jaycees, getting the word out about their involvement in cancer research. We were beginning to make things happen—we could see it—and that made a difference.

Another thing our presence was doing was bringing people out of their shells, providing a platform for them where they could speak openly about cancer. Almost everyone we met had a cancer story to tell —a family member, a friend, and in a surprising number of cases, even themselves—but they had never discussed it with strangers. Neither had we, for that matter, not until now, and they knew we cared and understood. It was clear from all this that many of the people in our audiences, were beginning to see cancer in a new light, understanding that open talk and public awareness were the great enemies of this killer, eventually leading to funding and research and a common determination to wipe it out. That was the theory and purpose behind the World Ride, and we saw that it was beginning to be a shared purpose. Our efforts were beginning to have an effect, and our awareness that many of these people would become involved in community efforts to fight cancer was heartening.

In the long run, a doff of the cap goes to Mr. A and Mr. B., who gave us all these good folks to talk to.

It was hard for us to say good-bye to St. Albans. Along with the encouragement of seeing our message get across, we'd made a lot of friends there, which turned out to be the case all over the world. Our pattern was to be in and out of towns in a few hours, meeting wonderful people, making friends, but never staying long enough to cement associations and enjoy them—which was sad. Even if we stayed a day or two, it was the same. We said our good-byes with regret in hundreds of towns across the world. It was definitely the down-side of the World Ride.

Oh, Canada!

Immediately after crossing the border, we took a wrong turn and got lost. Getting lost was becoming our specialty. At one rest-stop, Jeff fell asleep on a bench and so we left him there—what the heck. The French-speaking natives would be glad to give him directions. The thought of it made us hysterical.

Jeff caught up with us in due time, but what with getting lost and the wind picking up, it was clear we wouldn't make the Montreal press conference. There was just no accommodating Mr.A and Mr.B on this leg, so four of us held a little pow-wow. Our decision was to mark the spot where we were, load the bikes in Jim's van, drive the 35 miles to the press conference and then return the next day and resume biking from where we'd stopped.

That's what we did, bombing along over the speed limit, barely making it on time, but making it nonetheless and returning the next day to pick up where we'd left off.

The Montreal press conference was a new experience: Everything was big scale—reporters from big newspapers and big television stations. Whatever we said there went out to a lot of people—hundreds of thousands—and if there was ever a time to choose our words carefully and deliver our message clearly, this was the time and we all knew it.

Peter, being a Canadian, was the first to address the group and he really gave a super speech. It was exactly on target. I couldn't have been more delighted, and the audience loved it and loved him. And they loved the World Ride by the time he stepped down.

Following Peter's tour-de-force, we all had ample opportunity to give our individual views on things. Television crews filmed us in cycling formation in the parking lot, journalists took pictures, questions and answers flew back and forth—it was an exciting hubbub filled with good feelings all around. Indeed, the evening turned out to be one of the most pleasant and exhilarating of the whole trip. The one somber note was my remembrance of George Ash—who was never far from my mind—but now especially close in the city that he had many times declared to be his favorite. I wanted to reach for a phone and give him a call and say, "Hey, George, we're getting great press up here! Come on over!"

We spent a few days in Montreal, loving every minute of it and getting a chance to read our publicity and see ourselves on big-city television It was a great media city, and not a day passed when we weren't offered an interview or photo session, which we happily agreed to. Canada was the gateway to the world for us.

We spent one Montreal morning having our bikes tuned

up for free, and I traded in my forward-protruding handle-bars for handlebar extenders (protruding bars are typically used by racers, but mine couldn't be clamped and screwed down tightly enough and were slipping with even the slightest body weight).

Nancy came up June 25, which make Montreal positively paradise. We took some time for ourselves, knowing it would be the last we'd see of each other until she could arrange to come to Europe. Although it was glorious to have her beside me, it was painful beyond words to part when I boarded the plane to England.

All I could think of on the trip abroad was our last moments together, and I was halfway across the Atlantic before I could turn my attention to the great adventure that was about to unfold.

Four

THE ADVENTURE BEGINS

England: June 27–30

Many thousands of Americans have done overseas touring on bikes. It's a great way to really learn the culture of a foreign country, meet its people and have a terrific time while you're doing it. Most tourist bikers will cover a few hundred miles, maybe even a couple of thousand if they're really determined. Chances are they'll have planned their tour to cover the most lovely parts of the country or countries they're visiting—the Loire Valley in France, for example, or the Tuscany region in Italy. And then, when its over, they'll catch a plane and fly home, exhilarated by a marvelous vacation and memories to last a lifetime.

It's a little different when you set your sights on a 14,000-mile itinerary through 32 countries and some of the most rugged and inhospitable places on earth. This isn't a pleasant summer's tour; it's a serious adventure with equally serious liabilities and consequences.

Not All Post-Card Pretty

Given the ever-changing politics and inevitable social upheavals in such a wide-range of nations, there is no way of telling if you'll always be welcome where you're going or if you'll suddenly be involved in wars, riots, government take-overs or any of a dozen other unpleasant and danger-ous happenings. These are very real possibilities, and parts of our scheduling had to be changed as a consequence of exactly this sort of thing.

Some of the places we were headed for had 19th Century communications networks, primitive medical facilities, horse-and-cart road systems and straight up-and-down geography that would intimidate a mountain goat. Food supply was very "iffy" on many legs of the trip, repair facilities non-existent and language barriers in some rural places were impossible to overcome.

And while dealing with all of this, it was also necessary for us to adhere to our demanding schedule, which required us to be at certain places at certain times or risk inconveniencing people or blowing the whole mission.

So, it was a different kind of ride before us. Many peo-ple had warned us that our correspondence from our for-eign travels wouldn't consist of post-cards of pretty cathe-drals and vineyards, but rather, basic news that we were still alive.

More Kindness Abroad

We were reminded of none of the above, however, when we got off the plane at London, the essence of western civ-ilization. Met by a very British-looking pair, Corinna and Chris, who were sent by the Jaycees, we were immediately escorted into a dining room for scones and tea. Peter had ordered a bagel, which was no more a stock item in that restaurant than camel hocks, forcing him to join us in the scones.

After our little breakfast, we went to Chris's small car and we all knew right away that there was no way we'd get three bikes on or into it. So we arranged to store the bikes and some baggage at the airport for two days, and we were given the distinct impression that the storage would be free-of-charge. We were surprised at this and very pleased to see that kind of support for the mission—the same as we received in the U.S. and Canada. We had always figured that people everywhere would respond to the World Ride in pretty much the same way, but it was great to have confirmation within an hour of arriving in England.

Leaving the airport building, we headed for Chris's car and he suggested I ride in front. I started to get into the passenger seat, which turned out to be the driver's seat—the steering wheel in Britain being on the right. Chris thought my mistake was very funny, and so did I, but I didn't think it was funny at all when he swung out into traffic and drove down the left side of the street. I never did feel at ease in that car, and when we came to a busy traffic circle where everything was in reverse order, I nearly had a heart attack.

Somehow, we got to Chris and Corinna's house safely, and later they prepared a delicious barbecue for us. Peter promptly spilled a glass of wine and Jeff did the same with a bottle of barbecue sauce. Chris surveyed the damage and delivered the following in pure Laurence Olivier, "I say ... would you please spare the wedding presents?" There was no doubt that we were in England.

Exhausted from jet lag, I went to bed that night as soon as civilly possible and fell asleep with visions of biking over a hill on the wrong side of the road and being wiped out by a British truck or, rather, a "lorry."

Back to Work

The next day it was back to work. In the morning Jeff, Peter and I went to a bicycle shop to look for things we needed. Such shops are among the most omnipresent establishments in England, a country where biking is a national culture. We all agreed that this was a real bike shop. There were multiple bike posts for mechanical work, and every nook and cranny was jammed with bikes, parts, tools and every imaginable goody a cyclist could want—we just stood and gazed.

I looked at the prices and quickly changed my mind about needing a pair of sunglasses when I saw the English equivalent of a $50 price tag—which equaled my budget for four days.

It was fun observing British fashion and culture: bell-bottoms, platform shoes, red-linen telephone booths, super wide license plates on super small cars, school kids in matching suits and ties (or matching skirts and blouses), narrow sidewalks, Cockney speech— it was all interesting stuff. I suppose I could have explored things more, but I had work to do.

I had to send letters and faxes to Jaycees and Project Managers throughout Europe apprising them of our arrival and assuring them that we were on schedule, and that we'd confirm our itinerary as we neared their country. This had to be done before we began traveling again. I couldn't do all this and tour London at the same time. To tell the truth, I was anxious to get on with this business to avoid running into scheduling problems down the road.

So that's where my mind was. And added to this was the fact that Chris and Corinna—while they were wonderful hosts—had only known about us through the Jaycees. They hadn't invited us into their home because they longed for our company, but because they supported the World Ride and were doing their share to make it a success. When Chris returned home from work that evening, in fact, he saw my workload and volunteered a hand.

Other tasks attended to that day included acquiring bicycle maps of the United Kingdom and verifying road mileages (my original projections had been in error in some cases). We also brainstormed about how to get visas to enter Algeria.

The visa situation proved how much better it was to be a threesome on this World Ride rather than a twosome or foursome. Peter suggested obtaining the visas in Spain or Morocco, but this would have required us to spend time and money on trains to get to cities that were pretty far off our planned route. I wasn't too happy about the plan, and proposed that we extend our scheduled stay in Paris by a day. If we couldn't get the visas in Paris, we could then look at Spain and Morocco as alternatives. After hammering out the different approaches, Jeff eventually agreed to my plan and a decision was made. Peter didn't get upset or feel slighted, and neither did Jeff or I in succeeding months when decisions went the other way. Our democratic odd-man-out system was to serve us well on the World Ride and it averted friction on many occasions.

After dinner that night, Chris toasted us with some hard liquor brought in from Estonia, telling us we'd better get used to this stuff. Peter and I weren't drinkers, whereas Jeff was, but I downed one shot to honor the toast. Although I'm six-and-a-half-feet tall and weighed-in at about 225 pounds at the time, one shot did me in. Anyway, I'd had enough problems with Estonia without guzzling its booze—it was the one country I hadn't been able to reach by fax.

At one point before the evening ended, the phone rang and Corinna curled her finger at me, beckoning me over. It was Nancy.

On The Road Again

The next morning, following an early breakfast, we said our good-byes and piled into a taxi and drove to the airport to retrieve our bikes and extra baggage. True to the hopes we'd been given, there was no charge for the storage and we left with a few "Cheerios!" and "Good hunting, chaps!" ringing in our ears.

In good spirits, then, we wheeled our bikes through the airport to the adjacent train station and caught a ride to the outskirts of London where we were to begin our European tour. The name of the town, if you can believe it, was St. Albans—the namesake of the Canadian St. Albans we had recently toured.

More than just the starting point of the European tour, St. Albans represented the point when we were really on our own. We'd had three other cyclists riding with us in the U.S. and Canada—Maureen, Dan and Brian—and, of course, we'd had Jim in the support vehicle. Those days were finished. It was now just the three of us in a foreign country where nothing was familiar, where everybody drove on the wrong side of the road, where we had to get directions from a taxi-driver even to find our way out of St. Albans and where we were again faced with a strict schedule.

It didn't bother us, however. We were excited by the idea that we'd be in Hong Kong in four months, so why fuss about English roads that meandered off into nowhere now and then, void of signs? We'd learn to deal with it. Peter, at least, had biked in Britain before, not that he was familiar with our particular route, but he'd at least know some of the touring protocol.

Our first destination was Cambridge. I was running on crackers and peanut butter to save my budget, feeling weaker and weaker by the minute. About 20 miles up the road, my 21-gear bike started making a strange little noise. It kept increasing, and then my gears started to slip, first the medium gear, then the high and low gears. The bike was in real trouble so we pulled into the parking lot of a fast-food restaurant. Jeff was our mechanical guy—a near-genius at fixing bikes—and he took mine for a swing around the parking lot, going round and round while I pigged out at the restaurant. Overweight or not over-weight, budget or no budget, my eating regimen had to change if I was to survive the punishment of heavy-duty biking.

After an hour, Jeff temporarily repaired a chain ring that was about to bust. I got back on the bike and the repair lasted until we got within three or four miles of Cambridge, at which point my chain snapped. Jeff and Peter had been a good distance ahead of me, unable to hear my shouts, so there was nothing to do but walk it out.

Kings College had been our planned meeting place in Cambridge, and when Jeff and Peter arrived ahead of me and immediately got caught up in the excited business of filling everyone in on the World Ride, confident I'd be along at any time and not giving it another thought. I wandered in about a half-hour later, feeling about as physically miserable as it was possible to feel, and ended up having a photo taken of me holding up the broken chain.

All in all, it was an inglorious start to our great European adventure.

Five

MIRACLE WORKERS

Usually in a book of this sort an acknowledgment is given to those who helped make the story possible. This generally appears at the front of a book—as is the case here—but it's not enough in regard to the Jaycees. These people worked absolute miracles and they deserve a chapter of their own.

The Massachusetts Jaycees were the first to commit funds to the World Ride cause. They came in early with their commitment, which was subject to our obtaining a non-profit status, but the commitment was enough to encourage me and keep my plans alive.

But it wasn't just a cash commitment they gave. They gave me their influence with the U.S. Junior Chamber of Commerce, the Junior Chamber International and the Junior Chamber Senators. In other words, the Massachusetts Jaycees went to bat for me, persuading Jaycee organizations that I was worth listening to—that the World Ride Against Cancer was a cause worthy of Jaycee involvement and that I could be trusted to organize and fulfill the mission. In this way, and in many other ways, they kept the issue of the World Ride before the Jaycees and it resulted in my being invited to address the Junior Chamber International's Executive Committee in Coral Gables, Fl., in January of 1993.

A Jaycee known to the Executive Committee, Travis Ebel, had for some time shared my enthusiasm for the World Ride and he accompanied me to Coral Gables, supporting my presentation at every turn and arguing the case every bit as well as I could, and sometimes considerably better.

A World of Support

The result of our combined efforts was the Junior Chamber International's unanimous decision to support the World Ride Against Cancer. The support of the JCI, with its hundreds of Jaycee organizations in almost every country on earth, literally meant the world to me and the World Ride project.

From the day the World Ride began in Boston, to the day the World Ride ended in Boston—with a year and 32 countries in between—the Jaycees were our primary support system. They planned our routes so as to assure the presence of a local Jaycee organization at both ends, and usually in the middle as well. They set up our press conferences, arranged meetings with community leaders and hosted dinners for us. They often arranged accommodations for us at destination stops, such as with Chris and Corinna in London. They established a network of communications to keep tabs on our progress, our needs and our general well-being. On occasion, they even arranged for bike repairs and other necessities through their local contacts.

The World Ride, of course, had its own Board of Directors that was responsible for gathering and forwarding invaluable information to our Project Directors throughout the world. But even if we had had 10 times the personnel and facilities, we could not have done what the Jaycees did.

The logistics of the World Ride were staggering. Coordinating schedules in dozens of languages was, in itself, a challenge worthy of a major government's state department. And, in the beginning, I'm not sure that the World Ride team really believed things could possibly run smoothly.

Unwavering Presence

But at the end of tired day after tired day in the middle of far-off places whose names we sometimes couldn't even pronounce, there, right in front of us, right where they were supposed to be, right on time, were the smiling faces of Jaycees. After a while we stopped wondering if they'd be there—we came to be as sure of it as we were of the sun setting. Even to this day, when I ride a bike over to the next town, I sometimes find myself automatically expecting to meet a Jaycee up the road.

With the support of the JCI, and with our non-profit status in hand, the Massachusetts Jaycees funded $17,500 for air travel and for my per diem allowance, incidental expenses and administrative costs.

In my mind live the names of the many individual Massachusetts Jaycees who played a role in the success of the World Ride, as well as many of the hundreds of Jaycees throughout the world who were there when we needed them.

What the Jaycees supported was the fight against cancer—not me, but the cause I stood for. The cause was their motivation to stand on rainy street corners or at the end of dusty roads in numerous places spanning the globe looking for the first sign of our three-man team.

Six

ON THE "A" ROAD

England: July 1–8

Cambridge was a lovely town, much older than Boston, of course, but similar in architecture and ambiance, and I felt right at home. The whole atmosphere of Kings College and Cambridge, in fact, was young, vibrant, electric—full of fresh ideas and enthusiasm. Most of the movie, *Chariots of Fire*, had been filmed here and I'd recognized some of the locations as I'd walked into town—noting to myself that my dog-tired pace was a lot slower than the footracing seen in the movie.

The Jaycees led us on a grand tour of Kings College, arranged for us to wash up at a Jaycee's home and peg our tents on the lawn. They then took us to dinner that night in a local pub. We had a good time in Cambridge and I regretted that I couldn't indulge myself and hang around a few more days. Our schedule dictated the time we got up, where we went, when we went and how long it should take us to get there—and this occasion was no exception. We were due to arrive in Manchester in two days, a long route taking us through the busy heart of central England, and I had barely enough time the following morning to buy a new chain for my bike and get back on the road.

That road turned out to be an "A" road, and it provided a memorable few miles.

"A" Stands for Appauling

British "A" roads are the equivalent of our thruways—heavily traveled, high-speed and accommodating every class of vehicle. Some of the "A" roads were designed by normal, compassionate human beings who provided nice, wide shoulders for vulnerable cyclists. Other "A" roads, such as the one we were on, were designed by psychos who had been bumped by a bike in their childhood and thereafter sought to destroy every cyclist in Britain.

In no other place on the World Ride were we so constantly threatened with instant death. Trucks and semi-trailers had been fitted with kill-the-biker-radar. When we appeared on their screens, they started edging toward our side of the road, hurtling the rigs past us like missiles. We hugged the shoulder, which was an impossibly narrow path engineered for one-dimensional stick men. It was filled with debris, bike-bending bumps, overhanging branches and every other sort of obstruction designed to force us back into traffic. But we had no option, our survival depended on the mere inches of separation the shoulder provided.

At one of our nervous stops along this wild English road, we understandably got to talking about God and fate and such things, and what happens after death. After a few more miles of this Indiana Jones adventure it finally got to the point where our survival instincts were screaming at us so insistently that we turned off the "A" road and plotted a new course to Manchester. Throughout the ride, there were times when we disagreed about things—but not about that "A" road. No way.

Greener Pastures, Almost

Our new route was blessed in comparison, running through lovely English countryside and small towns.

My bike wasn't blessed, however, and started acting up again, precisely as it had done the day before, only this time with an added feature—a kinked rear wheel (reminding me of a revolving potato chip). This slowed me down considerably; Peter and Jeff rode on ahead while I plodded along as best I could. Because of my pace and the change we'd made in our route—and the certainty of my having to spend more time in a bicycle shop—it became increasingly clear that we wouldn't reach Manchester the following day. Having reconciled ourselves to the prospect, we kept on as long as we could and then headed for a campsite.

The first one that came into view was on a magnificent country estate owned by a gracious and charming older woman who was renting out tent space so she could earn enough to keep it. She was quite pleasant and we developed an instant rapport. Many once wealthy families in England have had to resort to opening up their castles and estates to tourists, charging entrance or camping fees or whatever else might bring in the cash needed to avoid the auction block.

It was a boon, of course, to wanderers such as us, but there was also a sadness about it. Our hostess, however, appeared anything but sad. In typical stiff-upper-lip British fashion, she bustled about the place in high cheer, acting like an employee of the estate rather than its titled owner. She even lent a hand fixing the water pipe I managed to break in her bathroom.

In the morning, after a solid 11 hours sleep, I walked to the road with my bike and flagged down a passing dump truck. The guys in the cab of the truck—David, Joe and Steve—were very cheery and pleasant and said it would be "no problem" to take me and the bike to the nearest bicycle shop. They asked me what sort of work I did, and I told them I was raising funds for cancer research by riding around the world. I could tell from their expressions that they figured I was rich and able to take a year off and go touring on a bike.

To get their curiosities on the right track, I told them my pay was zero, I'd spent almost all of my own money organizing the ride, that I was living on $11.50 a day (which was donated) and that I was doing it because I believed in the cause. They thought about all this for a moment and then concluded it was hilarious and we merrily bantered back and forth about this and other things for the rest of the trip.

Broken Bike Blues

The new wheel didn't end my problems, however. When Jeff, Peter and I resumed riding my gears continued to slip and Peter began to have his own bike problems. All considered, we reluctantly agreed that the only sensible thing to do was to officially abort our Manchester visit, get to a bike shop and have everything thoroughly and properly repaired. The Manchester Jaycees had set up a meeting with the Lord Mayor of Manchester, no less, but there was nothing we could do about it under the circumstances. It was going to take some time to repair the bikes, and if we still kept Manchester on our itinerary it would foul up the scheduling for a dozen other towns ahead. I called Andrew, the World Ride Project Manager in Manchester, to apologetically inform him of our change in plans.

It was not a happy call for me, I assure you. It was the first time I'd had to cancel a planned stop and I felt as if I'd failed the Jaycees and the World Ride, exhibiting a total lack of responsibility and leadership. The Manchester Jaycees, on the other hand, were completely understanding. Although their reassurance made me feel better, it didn't sweep away the guilt. A few days later, I would have to do the same thing again in Scotland, which created a double whammy of self-doubt.

Magnificent Martins

Andrew suggested I telephone a fellow Jaycee whose home was about eight or nine miles away from where we were. His name was Martin and he welcomed us royally. He took us to a pub that evening, and he and his wife, Sally, accommodated us, fed us with a huge English break-

fast the next morning and then sent us on our way—
stuffed, rested and happy. It was a great boost for my rock-
bottom spirits and a real respite from what had been a couple of really miserable days.

Leeds was our next destination, a long ride through hilly
English countryside (we saw hang-gliders at one point),
and Jeff's odometer informed us that we covered 93 miles
of the trip before being picked up in a van for the final 30-
plus miles to Leeds. (This was a pre-arranged pick-up by
another Martin, also a Jaycee.)

At this Martin's home we again were graciously waited-
upon, fed and housed. Martin apologized for not having
trimmed his hedge for our arrival and his wife apologized
for not having pressed our sheets. We were touched—they
had no idea of how we roughed it on the road and how luxurious their accommodations were to us. (A roommate in
their home, incidentally, was a disc jockey on a local radio
show and she took down the details of the World Ride and
promised to spread them to her listeners.)

A Year Older, A Lifetime Wiser

The next morning we were driven back to our pick-up
point where we were to begin our trek to York. On this leg
of the journey, spoke problems besieged Jeff and Peter so
we decided to split up—I would go onward to York while
they stayed to fix their bikes. Our plan was to meet up at
the York train station later, which we did, and then spent
the night in a youth hostel. It was the eve of my 31st birth-

day and Jeff bought me some sweet cider and peanuts. Peter shared his breakfast oatmeal with me the following morning—a real breakthrough for a guy who had told us at the very beginning of the ride that he never shared his food on bike tours.

I remember getting off by myself for a minute or two on my birthday and reflecting on my life. Despite the dismay I had felt over the Manchester fiasco, I realized how I was focusing my life on important work. That I believe in a good cause and was actually doing something about it, although I realized I had miles to go. I did know that there was really nothing else I'd rather be doing—the World Ride mattered to me just as Nancy mattered to me—it was that much a part of me. I could not have imagined not finishing it successfully.

Could We Really Do This?

Whether Jeff, Peter and I would be able to complete the World Ride as a team, however, I really didn't know. Equipment failure had become almost ongoing (we had to spend an extra day in York to acquire new wheels for Jeff's and Peter's bikes), patience occasionally ran short and adhering to a tight schedule was becoming a real threat to accomplishing a successful, timely ride.

The fundamental fault, however, was mine—and I don't say this to sound humble. I say it as a matter of fact. I was the one who had most of the equipment problems up to now, which had caused most of the delays; I was the one who had hastily chosen our bikes (swayed to a large extent by the discount I'd arranged) and all three of us were now paying the penalty. It was me who was still far from being in prime physical shape, not nearly as strong a rider as Peter or Jeff, and this was a cause of frustration when scheduling was particularly tight.

My reactions to daily aggravations were also less than ideal. Although held in check by my leadership role and the responsibility of keeping the mission running with a minimum of friction, I'm sure the demands I placed on the team caused resentment at times and that I didn't always come across with perfect tack. Add to all of this the following: Peter and Jeff had not been sponsored for the World Ride—each of them, as you'll remember, had coughed up $10,000 for the privilege of coming along with me. Also, they had nothing to do with designing our impossible itinerary—I had done that, also, albeit in league with the Jaycees. So when the timing for a leg was out of control, Peter and Jeff had a right to complain, I didn't.

Looking over the situation, and with the better part of a year of teamwork and togetherness still ahead of us, I seriously wondered if I'd have to end up finishing the World Ride by myself. At least the equipment problems would be cut by two-thirds and I wasn't worried about arguing with myself or dealing with myself diplomatically.

Riding alone, however, was the the very last thing I wanted to do, and the more I thought about it, the more certain I became that if we could solve the horrendous bike problems, it would solve about 90 percent of the frustration and friction. Despite our differences about things, we had come to like and depend upon each other more than any of us probably would have admitted. We had the right stuff to complete a successful mission, what we needed was the right equipment.

Coming out of all this heavy-duty thinking, I resolved to call Chris, our Project Manager for Scotland, and I told him we might be trading in our bikes when we got to Glasgow and that he should alert the folks there to our pending need. I also told him we'd be eliminating Inverness and Fort William from our Scotland itinerary, saving 135 miles of riding and making up for the time we'd spent on repair work in England. You can imagine how I felt about canceling another two stops!

More Bike Woes

Leaving York, of course, my bike promptly went on the fritz again and I had to spend more time in another bicycle shop. I remember ripping my bike bags off and throwing them on the ground when I first noted the new problem. To say I was angry is like saying that it's windy in a tornado.

Notes from my log, in which I did my best to enter daily details, recount a couple of more nights in English campgrounds ... more bike problems ... a 2,000-foot climb over the Pennine Chain (a range of hills extending from southern Scotland to central England) ... cold, misty weather ...

desolate, barren country ... another bike problem, Jeff and Peter ahead of me, as usual, so I couldn't call to them ... the bike mess so severe it required me to hitch a ride in a van to an upcoming town where I met up with Jeff and Peter ... bike repairs made ... Peter and Jeff going ahead once more ... my taking an "A" road after the repairs to make up for lost time ... the "A" road proving too dangerous ... switching to a side road and having no idea where Jeff and Peter were.

But who do I see after a mile or so on this side road? Jeff and Peter! Any lingering thoughts I had about doing this ride alone instantly vanished—I was never happier to see two people in my life than on that cold, rainy, lonesome road a few miles from the Scottish border.

We reached Dumfries, Scotland that evening—two days later than scheduled—each of us very conscious of the inconvenience we'd caused the Jaycees in Manchester and probably here as well. But here came Maureen, our Project Coordinator in Dumfries, cheerful as she could be, walking up to the Dumfries train station only 10 minutes after I had called and told her we'd arrived.

An awesome dinner was enjoyed by all, and Maureen played an answering-machine message from Nancy. Over the past few days, Nancy had called a couple of people in Scotland, not knowing about our most recent broken bikes and delays. She finally resorted to leaving a message on Maureen's machine.

"Hi, Maureen," the message said, "I want to wish

Richard a happy birthday. I'm his girlfriend and I love him very much."

It was a good ending to my week's tour of English bicycle shops.

Seven

FROM FIRTHS TO FJORDS

Scotland/England: July 9–19

The Firth of Clyde, the Firth of Lorne, the Firth of Forth ... the names of these deep, narrow inlets from the sea (called fjords in Norway) ring of Scotland as surely as highlands and bagpipes and kilts. A rugged and lonely landscape, yet spectacularly beautiful—given to great swings of moods in its valleys and hills and always beckoning the tourist to round the next bend. Such were the lofty musings I was to carry along with me on the Scotland tour, and my appreciation of the land was matched by my admiration for the hearts and minds of its people.

No sooner was it morning at Maureen's, when off we went to the Imperial Cancer Research Center in Dumfries to meet a photographer covering our story. (The ICRC was similar to our Salvation Army in that it raised money for research by accepting donations and selling goods.) Down-to-business interviews and meetings of this sort had been set up for us at all our stops in Scotland. Wherever we went, the Scots were perfectly organized; publicity was generous and hospitality and enthusiasm abounded. It was to be a tour of solid achievement for the World Ride mission and we were to come out of Scotland with refreshed convictions and a new readiness to take on the world.

Even our psychological warfare with the bikes diminished somewhat in Scotland. We decided to keep them a while longer, not wishing to take the time to haggle for trades when so many positive things were happening for the World Ride in such rapid succession. Actually, I speak more for Jeff and Peter here than for myself. Their bikes broke down only sporadically; mine was on the verge of it every minute—a source of continual concern on the remote roads of Scotland. But, by some magic, there always seemed to be a bicycle shop nearby and repairs were dealt with quickly and efficiently, keeping me going with a minimum of lost time. So I said a prayer and kept my bike.

One of the off-beat things we learned about the Scots had nothing to do with their efficiency and seriousness, but that some of them enjoy happy hour from dawn to dusk. We were on the road between Dumfries and Glasgow when we stopped at a bar for lunch, the only place in sight. It appeared that everybody in the bar was drunk—talking loudly, singing songs, their arms around each other. One woman, who walked at a 15-degree angle, took a fancy to Peter and Jeff, sidling over to them, feeling their legs and whispering things to them. I joined in on a couple of the songs and we soon tired of the scene so we said our good-byes and pedaled off with some new and entertaining memories.

Getting Us to Perth on Time

Glasgow had been chosen as the site for the 1995 JCI World Congress, a testament to its Jaycee activity. John, our principal Jaycee contact in that city, went out of his way to be helpful. From our first telephone call to him, he was eager to do anything he could to be of service to the team. He met us on the road as we entered Glasgow, for example, guiding me directly to a bike shop five minutes before it closed. Most extraordinary of all, he then offered to drive our bags to our next stop in Perth! He'd taken note of my conversation with the bike-shop owner and realized that if he took the bags our bikes would be 50 pounds lighter, relieving a great deal of stress on the wheels and spokes—the primary cause of our problems. Way to go, John!

He also suggested we take an "A" road to Perth to make better time. John was not a cyclist—he didn't know an "A" road from a biker's seat—and we told him bluntly that the "A" road would get us killed. We ended up taking other routes, most of them as narrow as the back roads in England, but we managed to maintain our pace of 13 to 14 mph, getting to our destination on time—which amazed John who was sure we'd be hours late.

Somewhere on the leg to Perth, we were sitting on a stone wall taking a break when we saw our first Scotsman in a kilt. We wondered why a grown man would prefer a skirt to pants, and I remember ending the conversation by saying that I didn't care what the Scots wore as long as they stayed just the way they were—which, to my mind, was terrific!

Also on the Perth leg, Peter was noticeably slower because of the pain in his back; he'd wrenched it at the hostel in York and it had become an increasing aggravation. Up until then, I had been the lone guy with aches and pains from being as out of shape as I was. Through Peter's pain, I sensed a sort of bonding going on between us, which I welcomed as being a good thing for the team.

Not Just Whistling Dixie

Jeff's very distinct whistle came in handy in Scotland. On the many occasions when I was delayed, the guys would go on ahead and we'd make plans to meet up again in a distant town. I'd arrive later without the faintest idea of where Jeff and Peter might be. There I was at dusk, standing in the rain, and suddenly out would come Jeff's whistle from some alley—shrill, very different from any other sound—and all I had to do was to follow the whistle to find him. Simple as that. A real useful talent. I had taken advantage of his whistle in the States, in Canada and England, but the welcome sound of it in the misty, remote places of Scotland is clearest in my mind.

We hit the 1,000-mile mark on our way to Perth and the Perth Jaycees met us on the road with a big sign to celebrate the event. One of them borrowed my camcorder and recorded the occasion for my future grandchildren. (I'd been using my camcorder and a still camera to document the World Ride from start to finish, and I eventually ended up with some 15 hours of video tape and 700 slides.)

Saint John, as I came to think of him, had not only driven our bags from Glasgow to Perth, giving our bikes a new lease on life, but he had also arranged for Bob—another Jaycee—to drive them 90 or more miles to Aberdeen, the next leg of our trip. A saintly man, indeed, was John, whose title I now conferred upon Bob as well.

I played mind games on long legs like this, splitting the run up into 20-mile segments. It doesn't seem so long and forbidding that way (20 miles to go, 19 to go, 18, etc., rather than 90, 89, 88, and so on). It always works, so I pass it along—although I didn't really need to encourage myself with the trick on this leg. I saw some guys bungee-jumping with nothing but hard Scottish rock beneath them. There's no way I would have traded even a grueling 90-mile bike ride for an afternoon of doing what those guys were doing.

In The Fast Lane

Like to drive a car real fast? Well, here's a story for you. I felt guilty for canceling our stops in Inverness and Fort William, and when the opportunity came up to make a proper apology I jumped at it. Anne Murray, the International Director for the Jaycees in Scotland, and our primary contact in Aberdeen, had arranged a press conference for us at the Aberdeen Royal Hospital. During that conference I learned that the President of the Inverness

Jaycees would be attending a Chamber meeting in a near-by town. A woman named Lindsey, who was Peter's host in Aberdeen, offered to drive me over. We headed out on a two-lane country road and it soon occurred to me that we were motoring along at a pretty good clip. Looking at the speedometer, I saw the pointer at 110 mph. Not kph, mind you, but good old American mph.

Not wanting to appear chicken in the face of certain death in the next second or so, I casually remarked, "My, my, look at that, a hundred and ten. What, uh, what sort of speeding fines do they have in Scotland?"

"About 575 pounds at this speed," she said.

"Really?" I said, as we passed an entire Scottish farm in a moment's blur, "Why that's about $750 in my money. "

She pondered that for a moment or two. "Yeah, it is, isn't it?" And with new insight she slowed down enough that the countryside came back into focus.

We got to the meeting and I made my apology, which was accepted with grace. The Inverness Jaycees were very important to the Junior Chamber International (the JCI, you'll remember, was the group I had spoken to in Coral Gables in January, coming away with their support for the World Ride). Inverness, however, was in the far northern reaches of Scotland, and because of my bike problems and the need to make up lost time, I had to strike it from my itinerary. I'd felt rotten about it and I accepted that evening's suicidal drive as fair and proper atonement.

Our bikes were repaired free of charge in Aberdeen. Anne rewarded the bike-shop owner for his generosity by arranging for a photojournalist from a large local newspaper to interview the team at the bike shop—a nice bit of unexpected publicity for him.

Scottish businessmen have a stereotyped reputation for stingy dealings and this is as misleading as any other stereotype. There was only one instance of this behavior during our entire tour of Scotland—it happened at a rural restaurant where the manager threatened to send me back out into the rain unless I ordered something. With that one exception, I can think of no more generous, giving people than those who everywhere extended themselves on our behalf in that delightful country. The only thing that's chilly in Scotland is the climate.

Remember Bob, the fellow Jaycee whom Saint John had recruited to drive our bags from Perth to Aberdeen after John had driven them up from Glasgow? Well, Bob didn't stop at Aberdeen. This member of the Board of the Junior Chamber of Scotland hung around town and then drove our bags on to Dundee, our next stop. Nobody paid him for this. No deals were made. He did it out of sheer human kindness. Here is your true Scotsman.

The Reason We Ride

Gramby Television gave us some fine publicity the next morning in Aberdeen, and then we were off and rolling to Dundee and to what we were told was Europe's largest hospital. A new wing was being opened for cancer research, and we were to be a part of the ceremonies.

While there, we learned from one senior cancer researcher that less than 25 percent of cancer research funding in the United Kingdom is provided by the government, the rest comes from private sources. As a consequence, their research tends to focus on basic discovery. They don't have enough money to select one or two theories and then pour millions into follow-up experiments. I sensed this researcher's dismay that the Americans didn't consult more frequently on basic findings before allocating huge sums to avenues of research that the Dundee researchers had found less than promising.

During our visit to Dundee, The Lord Mayor presented us with a sizeable check for the World Ride's cancer crusade and we taped a news brief for the local radio station and its 400,000-plus listeners.

Our next stop was St. Andrews—the golfing Mecca of the world—and here, as in many places, both local Jaycees and other interested individuals would often ask to ride along with us for a few miles. They rode mostly because they enjoyed it, but also to have a part in the World Ride. This was fine with us, and company was always welcome, but my physical condition and stamina had increased a dozenfold over the first few weeks and it was a challenge for me—to say nothing of Jeff and Peter—to keep our speed down to accommodate the casual bikers who couldn't begin to keep up with what had become our standard pace.

Edinburgh was our last stop on the U.K. portion of the World Ride, and once again the Jaycee people were totally generous and supportive. As I close the U.K. tour, I'd like to note that a majority of the people we came in contact with throughout the World Ride—and it seemed especially so in Scotland—had experienced the decimation of cancer in their families. Their support for the World Ride was as genuine on that level as on any other, and I understood how sincerely these people wished us well and how much they were counting on the success of the World Ride to raise awareness and funds for cancer research.

I realized as we put our bikes and bodies on the train for Newcastle, England, that it was a serious business, this World Ride.

And it was with such sobering reminders in my head that I boarded the ferry to Bergen, Norway, a day later, being immediately surrounded by a mixture of unintelligible Scandinavian conversations and becoming aware for the first time that we were truly stepping off into whole new worlds of challenge.

Eight

MIDNIGHT RIDING

Norway/Sweden/Finland:
July 20–August 9

I was thinking about Vikings as we neared the Norwegian coast— huge, bearded, daring warriors with horned helmets and mighty swords setting out in dragon boats to pillage England, or cross the Atlantic to discover new worlds. With such an ancestry, I wondered what the people would be like. Words like hard, austere and cold came to mind.

These were my thoughts as the ferry pulled into Bergen harbor, but after one look at Trimm they never again entered my head. Here was a happy-looking young guy in light summer clothes eagerly holding up a World Ride poster and showing the excitement of a pup when he spotted us. On his car was another World Ride poster and he even presented us with World Ride T-shirts made up especially for our visit. Trimm was the World Ride Project Manager in Bergen, and his was the kind of modern, bright, super friendly personality we were to encounter everywhere in Norway. No war helmets, just baseball caps.

Right away he guided us to the center of town where the Jaycees had a big gathering going on in our honor complete with a stage and a big banner reading: JUNIOR CHAMBER BERGEN WELCOMES WORLD RIDE AGAINST CANCER. We were celebrities! Live music was being played by a couple of guys from a band with one of its songs on Norway's Top Ten—these noted musicians were a guaranteed magnet for everybody who passed. Chairs and a microphone had been set up for us on the stage and, Trimm, acting as interpreter, got questions and answers going between us and passersbys. It was crazy. It was terrific. It was Norway. That's how it started the moment we stepped off the ferry.

A Fine Norwegian Night

On that first night, having to ride to a town more than 70 miles beyond Bergen, we rode in daylight until 10:15 p.m.—the sun setting in a brilliant fireball, spectacularly beautiful, like nothing I've ever seen. For another hour we rode on in a soft, lovely dimness, not like dusk, but different—there was something strange, wonderful and magic about it—like a ride in after-shadows. As bone-tired as I was, and dreading the thought of a grueling cross-country haul after an uncomfortable sleep on the floor of the ferry, I was entranced by the sheer beauty of the night—a truly exquisite experience in a strange and far-away land.

We rode for hundreds of miles in Norway, across angular and rugged landscape that was flecked with little towns nested in the foot of the cliffs. No wide panoramas here, but a lot of cliffs and towns. There were a lot of tunnels—

straight and curving—that ran through the hills. Along the coast, we were forever ferrying across fjords with little storybook towns on either sides—brightly colored, filled with small shops, clean, tidy, no sign of poverty anywhere.

Although modern in every sense and totally attuned to the world, Norwegians are very much in touch with their heritage. Not so much the Viking part (which they view somewhat in the qualified way we view our taking of the West from the Indians), but rather with the other ancient makings of their society and character. Wonderfully social on the outside—we passed up many parties to keep on schedule—they are conservative on the inside. Like New Englanders, they are proud, practical and have a wry sense of humor. One feels a great solidness here, a sureness about things. If there is a soft spot in this stability, it's in their economic dependence upon oil. Although they have a lot of it at the moment, their reserves are expected to run out in 50 years. One man said to me, however, that when Norway runs out of oil, it will tap its natural gas resources, which it has an abundance of as well.

Maybe he's right. But it was unsettling to me to note such a dependence on any one thing by a people that seemed the most independent of any I'd met.

Like Heroes and Kings

As in Scotland, the Jaycees were everywhere we went and press conferences and interviews abounded in small towns and large. We never lacked a gracious host, even being treated to a two-night stay in a hotel that catered to the Norwegian royal family. More than once we dined on shrimp, caviar and salmon sandwiches. Our advance publicity was terrific. Everybody knew we were coming long before we got there—not just the Jaycees, but whole towns. We rode into these towns dirty, tired and bedraggled, but we were welcomed like heroes and treated like kings.

The only really off-beat experience we had in Norway was at a Jaycee meeting on a town dock where a drunk came up to Peter and said, "You Americans stole all the Indians' land and killed them off." Peter was Canadian, of course, and he said so to this guy, but he continued accusing Peter and then walked off only to get into a wrestling match with the cop who had led us—on his bike—into town for the Jaycee welcome party with the Mayor. The cop didn't have a gun, but he did have a walkie-talkie, and the drunk grabbed it and threw it into the bay, at which point he was handcuffed and led to a paddy-wagon. I have a feeling that the tossing of the walkie-talkie was an exceptionally bad idea. I saw a little bit of the Viking in the cop's face as he watched his radio go sailing into the water.

Team Troubles

Despite the joy of Norway, my relationship with the team, particularly with Jeff, was coming apart. My bike situation, our relentless schedule and our shared exhaustion was becoming intolerable. The wheels on my bike were literally falling to pieces, spokes flying off continually and causing countless repair stops. Nowhere else had we kept to an itinerary as demanding as the one we were following here, and Jeff's increasing impatience with any delay—compounded by my own impatience with my bicycle problems and the delays they were causing—caused many testy moments between us. The Jaycees had expended themselves on our behalf in Norway and our diplomacy had to be perfect, which meant attending functions when we'd have preferred to rest for a few hours. Also, my administrative work and coordination efforts kept us off the road when we might otherwise have been riding. Add the necessity of my bike repairs to this mix of delays, as well as the time I spent on a renewed search for a new bike, and the time situation was getting out of hand. Even unflappable Peter had finally lost it with our demanding itinerary. "Call our Swedish contact," he shouted at one point, "and tell him not to ride us so hard! We'll burn out at this rate!"

Jeff and I agreed with him. And all three of us had also come to the unhappy conclusion that we probably wouldn't be getting any rest until the ride was completed in June of 1994, since Peter had only a year's leave from the Canadian military. He summed up what we all felt when he said that it was the socializing at night that was killing us. In short, things had to change—it was simply becoming too much to bear.

New Bike, New Outlook

Things began to change a few days later. An Oslo bike dealer who knew of my wheel troubles offered to donate a new bike to the World Ride cause. The bike was a touch small, but it was light-years better than the one I had and I accepted it in an instant with the gratitude of a man rescued from quicksand.

My new bike went a long way toward improving the team's compatibility. In fact, on our 161.9-mile journey to the Swedish border, I beat Peter and Jeff to the first stop by 10 minutes. Now, that was a switch!

The trip to the Swedish border and, in fact, throughout Sweden, was laden with almost constant rain—cold, hard and penetrating northern rain that soaked us to the bone and made our brief Swedish tour excruciating. The longest leg of the World Ride, we left Oslo at 9 a.m. and arrived in a small Swedish town about 60 miles outside of Goteborg, Sweden, at about 11 p.m.

By the time we had reached the border, I had become totally unfit for another foot of riding. A fever had taken over my body, the onset of what was probably the flu, and I was completely exhausted. My throat was sore and my bones and muscles ached ferociously.

At the border we were met by Jon (pronounced "Yawn"), our Swedish contact , who made it very clear that the Goteborg Jaycees were expecting us by 1 p.m. the following day. If we were to make it on time we'd have to ride another 70 miles or so before bedding down for the night. Apparently, the Goteborg Jaycees had arranged a huge welcome for us—pictures of me and announcement signs of our arrival had been posted all over Goteborg. Many Jaycees and political bigwigs had been invited. It was a major event in which a lot of time and energy had been invested—there was no way we could let these folks down. No matter what, we had to log those 70 or so miles before putting the day to bed. Jeff and Peter weren't ill, but they were cold, soaked and dead tired.

Somehow, however, we managed to do it, crashing eventually in a flea-bag hotel in some town whose name I was too tired to record. The next morning, with what must have been Divine help, I managed to get up, force my way through a newspaper reporter's questions and then join the team for a timely arrival in Goteborg. The President of the Goteborg Junior Chamber met us and, very apologetically, told us that the welcome ceremony and meeting had been canceled.

On The Mend in Sweden

That day and the next day, a very ill World Ride team leader was housed by a very accommodating Jon, inspected by a doctor and allowed to sleep at will. The cancellation of the Goteborg ceremonies had just been one of those things—I'd had to cancel a few planned stops of my own in England and Scotland, you'll remember. But other arrangements for publicity from Goteborg to Stockholm were to be kept as scheduled and the hospitality, dedication and enthusiasm of the Swedish Jaycees was everything I could have wished for.

While I was resting in Goteborg for the day, Jeff and Peter had gone ahead. Thinking of them cycling without me caused me to again consider my vulnerability. I had visions of getting really sick in some third-world country and being called off the World Ride, flown home for medical treatment, the mission canceled, and so on and so on.

The following morning, with my bike on a roof-rack and medicine in my pocket, I was driven to Jonkoping to meet up with Peter and Jeff. The doctor had told me to take great care not to exert myself with bicycling, but our itinerary wouldn't allow that, so we continued to cycle at full throttle to keep up with our intense schedule. I bundled myself up warmly under a fine raincoat and headed off on the next leg with Peter and Jeff. Dick and Betty Lutts, friends from home, had sent me some Shaklee vitamins and I armed myself with a pocketful.

Downpours continued on our route for the next couple of days, right through to Stockholm, where we picked up visas for Russia and then boarded a ferry for Turku, Finland.

If that seems to be a very short and unfair account of our Swedish tour, I'm afraid there's little else I can tell you. I couldn't see the land through the rain; I couldn't focus on personalities or perceptions through the fever and exhaustion; and my notes and memories contain very little, except for the kindness of individual Jaycees and other Swedes. We paid for almost nothing there—food and lodging being generously offered at every turn, and publicity for the World Ride and it's fundraising efforts for cancer was prominent in several of the towns we visited. Our Swedish ride covered only about half the miles we'd covered in Norway. I have often wished I could go back and start the Swedish tour all over again, healthy this time and wide awake. And, hopefully, in a dry spell.

Finishing Up in Finland

Finland was to be our shortest European tour. From Turku to Helsinki, we rode 110 miles in all. Again, it was mostly in the rain and little of the countryside could be seen, but every mile was filled with affirmation of the pleasantness of northern people, very much like those we'd met in Norway and Sweden—helpful, courteous, open, respectful, happy to give us directions and positively forthcoming with advice about our upcoming travels to Russia and the Baltic States.

Helsinki is very modern and western in its look and feel. Its citizens have a particular affinity for saunas. During a visit to an insurance company, the manager proudly showed me around the place, at one point opening a door to a sauna—it was part of the office much like a mail room is part of an American office. I thought I'd suggest it to my insurance agent in Boston.

Most striking about the Finns is their spirited love of their country and their great pride in its accomplishments. As Americans, Jeff and I were two or three times reminded by the Finns of how their country had been the only nation to fully repay its debt to the U.S. after World War I. Their national pride seemed to derive in great extent to Finland's heroic defense against the Russians in World War

II. On several occasions, conversations would invariably come around to that subject—the Finns never missed an opening to bring it up.

Would you believe that we found Tex-Mex food at a restaurant half-way between Turku and Helsinki? We did! In fact, the whole place was decorated in American south-west trappings.

Somewhere around this Tex-Mex stop, I had another spoke problem. Though the spoke problem with my new bike was 1,000 percent less frequent than it was with my old one, I hadn't completely eliminated it. My thoughts immediately moved ahead to the Russian and Baltic part of the World Ride—where I had no idea what would be available in terms of repair facilities. I determined it would be a good move to get an extra 10 or 12 spokes in Helsinki to carry as spares. Self-sufficiency would be a valuable asset in the days ahead, and we all knew it and prepared for it as best we could.

It wasn't bike repair, however, that we were being continually warned about by our Finnish friends. They were concerned about our personal safety. They were so insistent and dramatic—telling us stories ranging from instant arrest to tourists being shot to death by insane Russian women—that I thought it best for us not to listen. The Norwegians and the Swedes had suggested we listen to the Finns about these places—Russia and the Baltic States (Estonia, Latvia and Lithuania), but it was so excessively negative that I deemed it best that we not hear it on the eve of our departure.

The Finns, we concluded, had a flare for the dramatic. A Helsinki cancer organization, in fact, had the wildest anti-smoking campaign I'd ever seen. They had a slogan for their promotional material—IF YOU SMOKE, YOU CAN'T POKE. They directed this embarrassment toward 18- to 25-year-old males. The slogan definitely made me uncomfortable, but perhaps some people will live longer because of it. Apart from written literature, they also prepared this campaign for airing in public movie theaters.

On To Russia

This completes my notes on our very short—too short—tour of Friendly Finland. Helsinki, of course, where the anti-smoking film is knocking them dead at the box-office, was our last destination and it was here that we boarded the train for St. Petersburg, Russia. We only had four-day visas and couldn't afford the time to bicycle from Helsinki to St. Petersburg. On the plus side, however, we figured we'd escaped a day's ride in cold, drenching rain. But guess what? It stopped raining. As bad luck would have it, instead of riding under a luxuriously warm, bright, sunny sky, we were locked in a train!

The other thing that caught us by surprise was the loss of our passports. The Russian officials on the train immediately took them without a word of explanation. A Finnish conductor assured us the passports would be returned and that we shouldn't worry. He was right, but we had experienced our first taste of the official suspicion and paranoia that we were to encounter everywhere in the next several days. It was just the opposite of what we had experienced up to now, and we did not look forward to it.

Nine

COUNT YOUR BLESSINGS

Russia/Estonia/Latvia/Lithuania:
August 9–20

Our journey through Russia and the Baltic States was a dangerous and unpleasant 600-mile tour. Communism reversed the technological and social progress of these peoples to a mid-19th Century level and the sight of it was astounding.

In one short train ride we had come from a thoroughly modern, open, developed civilization to one that was barely capable of grasping the concept. It was like riding over the hill from a pleasant visit with friends who shared your values into a scene that could have been set by Charles Dickens—dull, grimy towns and children guarding borders with AK-47s. Suspicion, distrust and poverty were everywhere. It was a place where we deliberately grew scraggly beards and let the mud and dirt from rain-filled pot holes stay on our faces so we might look more threatening and avoid attack and robbery.

It's hard to imagine how these people are ever going to climb out of generations of social, economic and technological stagnation. But some of them are trying—rushing awkwardly but determinedly into new-found freedoms.

We saw a clean, bright, American-style convenience store in the middle of a block of grotesquely dirty buildings and knew that the owner of that store is trying. The man who built a swimming pool and tennis court at a local entrepreneur's home in the heart of a soot-covered town desperate to attract tourists also is trying. The local businessman who begged for information that might lead to profitable business ideas is trying, too.

But we're talking about entire populaces—whole countries stuck somewhere between the Middle Ages and the Industrial Revolution. In Estonia, for example, you can't make an out-of-country call without going to a central Telephone/Telegraph agency. There are countries where you can get a room for $3.50 a night; countries where you buy your food from kiosks along the road from kerchiefed peasants; countries where I drank nothing but warm soda off the shelves (no refrigerated machines anywhere) rather than trust the tap water; and countries where our western bikes were equivalent to a year's wages—and eyed as hungrily. Less than 50 miles away, across the Gulf of Finland, the other world and its economies, customs, know-how, conveniences and comfortable, non-threatening lifestyles seemed impossibly out of reach. How many generations would it take to catch up and attain these things?

Probably a lot fewer than I might think, given the new independences and emerging fervor of the people—but how hard it is going to be!

On the Road to Capitalism

Sergei was our World Ride Project Manager in St. Petersburg and he'd been the 1980 Olympic Gold Medalist winner in swimming. He made his living importing Jeep Cherokees. He'd bought four or five with an American partner and sold two, and the one he met us in had no license plate. It was totally illegal, but the times were changing in Russia and it was every man for himself. As Peter put it, "It's a lawless society and a guy like Sergei can get away with it."

Sergei had a nice apartment. He was one of the precious few who could be called upscale—nobody else we met seemed to have a dime and they were trying to figure out how to make it in Russia's newly evolving capitalistic system. After nearly 80 years of being taught the venality of capitalism, their tunnel-vision view was that it operated on the simple basis of getting what you could. Mutual trust and the sanctity of negotiated deals—which is what makes most of capitalism work—was still unknown.

Through his many newspaper contacts as a sports celebrity, Sergei arranged some good publicity for the World Ride and its anti-cancer mission. After the interview, one of the photographers agreed to take some personal photos of the team for 50 cents a print. The next day when he delivered the prints, the price had doubled to a dollar. Sergei told the photographer that the team didn't mind the price—whether 50 cents or a dollar, it was still a bargain—

but we had made a deal at 50 cents and were dismayed with his lack of ethics. This was a new concept to the budding capitalist photographer.

From St. Petersburg, we rode in the rain directly to the Estonian border, less than 100 miles away. We negotiated countless pot holes overflowing with whatever substances Russian and Estonian tankers decided to drop on the road—some sludge here, toxic waste there. Looking at the terrible condition of the road and the impoverished appearance of everything else, the suspicious contents of those pot holes made us very conscious that our health was as much on the line on this trip as our lives. After my lunch of cookies and soda from a kiosk—the only food that seemed to be available—we passed through customs (only 30 minutes, thanks to Sergei's influence) and entered Estonia.

Braving the Baltics

We had no Jaycees to meet in Estonia, no scheduled meetings or deadlines. We saw no bike shops, and lived mainly on candy, bread and soda. We stayed at hotels where they locked the doors behind us and we appeared to be the only three people in the country who spoke any English. The standard of living here was even lower than in Russia, and we watched our bikes and cameras with exceedingly great care, taking turns at standing guard when the others went into shops or other establishments. Tough-looking kid gangs were common and it wasn't unusual to be directly approached for a handout of some kind.

Alex MacDonald, JCI Vice President for Europe, had asked me to meet with a group starting a cancer hospital in Tartu, the second largest city in Estonia. I'd promised him I would, but no contact could be made when I got to Tartu and I was very unhappy about it. Alex had extended himself to set up the World Ride throughout Europe—I was deeply indebted to him—and I couldn't fulfill this one, simple promise I'd made (though there was comfort in having tried). Just outside of Tartu, we somehow got in with a group of older women that was part of a larger group from 23 countries; they were holding a convention near that city. "Why in the world," I asked in amazement, "would a women's group convene in Estonia of all places?" One of the women said it was because it was cheap.

Estonia had brought out the worst in us and it was at an Estonian campground that the antagonisms between Jeff and me came to a head and we had it out. He accused me of being the ugly American, living in the past, not being a part of nature—and he was probably right. I accused him of being on sabbatical and looking for fun, whereas my family had been wrecked by cancer. I had spent two years of my life organizing this World Ride to fight back, I didn't get into it for fun and games, and said that while I had opposite ideas from his, I was just as right as he was.

This confrontation in the Estonian woods was probably the best thing that happened in the Baltics. It aired out mutual grievances, giving a healthy vent to them, and it emphasized our need for interpersonal skills and patience. Things between us were a lot better after that and the team was the beneficiary. Jeff was a good team member, witty and bright, and it was a pleasure to enjoy him without hidden resentments.

There were no AK-47s at the Latvian border, as there had been at the Estonian/Russian border—the Estonians and Latvians apparently got along a lot better than the Estonians and Russians. We took photos of a surprisingly friendly Latvian guard and he took photos of us. At a restaurant that night, we met a man who had grown up in Latvia, but later made his home in England. He said this was his second time back since World War II and that Latvia hadn't changed. We believed him. Another man offered to rent us lodgings for the night. No hot water, though. We turned him down.

Many, many people were selling wild mushrooms, which they had picked from the woods along the roadside. The poverty is very deep here and, not surprisingly, alcoholism—the bar-smashing kind—was evident everywhere. The language barrier was a severe and constant problem. For example, a Boston radio station had asked me to call them from Latvia to report on the World Ride progress, but the operator at the Telephone/Telegraph Agency couldn't understand how to handle my request for reverse charges and I had to let it pass.

Lithuania was the same as Latvia—which was the same as Estonia—and except for the usual traffic back-up at the border (we were always allowed to go to the front on our bikes), there was no visible evidence of our having crossed into this last of the Baltic States. Interestingly, not once in the Baltics was our baggage checked. This was inconsistent with the suspicious nature of Baltic officialdom and we never could explain it.

We went into a bank to cash a traveler's check and the uniformed guard was carrying an AK-47. We saw an American-type ice cream shop with a banana split displayed on a colorful sign and rushed in to get one, eagerly pointing to the split and salivating at the thought. I was given an ice cream cone instead. At another place, I tried my best to get a half-kilogram of baloney, not a kilogram, but it was the kilogram I got.

There were lots of children around in the cities, dirty, unkempt and street-wise, with few parents to be seen. They reminded me of characters from *Oliver Twist*. I took some pictures of them. Food in restaurants invariably was limited, invariably greasy; diarrhea accompanied me on a good part of the Baltic tour.

A Different Kind of Camp

On our biking map, there was a campground symbol next to the southern Lithuanian city of Kaunas. This campground turned out to be the site of a Nazi death camp in which 30,000-50,000 Jews had been slaughtered. Some were from Lithuania and some from other occupied countries who'd been brought in for the killing. Unaware of any of this, we entered a grey building on what appeared to be the campground site designated on our map and we asked a woman where we might pitch our tents for the night. This building housed the Administration Office for the historical site and the woman we'd met was the Curator.

Kindly offering us lodging in the Administration building, she then led us on a tour of the grounds—and nothing that has ever occurred to me in my life was to affect me so profoundly or haunt me so indelibly as that hour's walk through the death camp at Kaunas.

Coming up over a grassy knoll that looked like a well-kept park, we stumbled upon an old, weather-beaten brick building, which appeared to be a remnant of another time. Several yards away from the building stood an equally weathered concrete wall, with a cobblestone walkway in between. As we came closer, we saw that these things had been preserved from the Kaunas death camp.

The wall was a "killing wall." It was against this buttress of concrete that the camp's prisoners had been lined up by the Nazis and shot. The countless bullet-holes had been preserved, as though they had been made that morning. The height of the holes bore terrible testimony to the killing of children as well as adults. I was numb over the horror of what had happened here, and could respond to nothing for several minutes. I was enveloped in emotions I had never known.

Two signs were attached to the wall telling of the killing and of the nearby burning of the bodies. One of the signs was in English, as if to say to people like me, "Please understand this. You were not here, but this happened.

Read and remember. We say this in your own language so that you will know. It is only you who can stop it from happening again. Please remember us."

The cobblestone walkway between the wall and the building was called "The Way of Death" and I walked every step of it, filming it as the 30,000 to 50,000 men, women and children had walked it—from the building to the wall.

The building, itself, was the prison—left exactly as it was, meticulously preserved, unpainted and unwashed, dusty, indescribably haunting—everywhere revealing the names of prisoners etched into the rough plaster on an inside wall during their last hours of life. The Curator told us that on December 25, 1941, 64 prisoners successfully escaped by making 360 adjoining holes with a hand-made drill and had then fled into Kaunas to join the resistance against the Nazis. In the prison there were newspaper clippings testifying to the extraordinary work of a Japanese diplomat stationed in Lithuania during the war, who had somehow managed to provide visas to hundreds of Lithuanian Jews, saving them from being sent to this death camp—a Japanese Schindler. There was a huge amount of testimony to this man, and I regret that I neither remember nor did I record his name. In Lithuania, however, it is revered.

On May 20, 1993, just a few months before we'd arrived at this death camp, a visitor went into the prison and saw a prisoner's name that he recognized as being his father's! His father was taken by the Nazis, he'd never known what had happened to him. Now he knew—it was etched in the wall of the prison at the death camp in Kaunas.

If you're planning any kind of trip through eastern and northern Europe, you should visit a concentration camp and feel the presence of all the innocent lives that were taken. I assure you that you will be moved in a way you've never experienced and will come away from such a place a different person than the one who entered.

Ten

BACK TO THE WEST

Poland/Germany:
August 20–September 9

Leaving Lithuania and entering Poland, we began our transition back to the familiar things of the West. The change wasn't immediate, but it became more noticeable with every mile.

Bread lines gradually disappeared and the food supply became more predictable and plentiful. The towns were neater and cleaner (we often saw lovely flower beds in highway divider strips), western-style clothing was more common and merchants were using cash registers and other electronic devices rather than abacuses, which we had seen frequently in the Baltics. English was more widely spoken, faces were friendlier and we had a growing assurance that should something happen to us here—a medical emergency, for example—reasonably competent help would be available. After 150 miles or so into Poland, traveling inward from Suwalki, we had the distinct sensation of having returned to the West—it felt wonderful.

The Hub of Eastern Europe

Poland was the showcase for Eastern Europe. It was showing its neighbors how to evolve from social and economic suppression. This evolution hadn't yet spilled over into the Baltic States, but as the fear of Russia subsides and the awareness of the outside world increases, I have no doubt the people will adapt their many skills to assure their share in a far better life than they've had. They've almost missed an entire century, and Poland is showing them how to begin to catch up.

It was in Poland that I occasionally began to take the lead position in our riding. I'd lost about 20 pounds and hardened up remarkably. When I met Nancy several days later in Berlin, she was shocked at my weight loss, convinced at first sight that I was ill. It was during one of these leads, riding hard, that I bounced over a railroad track, eventually breaking a spoke and sending my wheel out of whack. Bicycle shops weren't easily available, but I was told about a man who repaired mopeds in his backyard garage—like many lawn mower repairmen in the U.S.—and I went to him and he trued (straightened) my wheel. He was a pleasant guy with plenty of ingenuity, and seemed headed toward a full-fledged business. Poland isn't quite there yet, but was well on its way. Unlike the Baltics, there was a feeling of hope rather than resignation.

Jeff and I were continuing to get along well and the three of us were making a better team. In part, it was the improving environment, but I think it was also due to my decision to stop micro-managing our personal affairs and quit worrying so much about our relationships. Instead, I concentrated on the mechanics of staying on schedule. It was the World Ride that counted, and the looser I became about peripheral matters the better things seemed to go. I thought a lot about spending time with Nancy in Berlin, and I was looking forward to coordinating things with the Jaycees. We hadn't seen a Jaycee since Finland and wouldn't see any until Poznan, our last major destination in Poland.

On To Poznan

Poznan is about 50 miles from where we were to cross into Germany and it was by far the most western of Poland's cities. It was on the road to Poznan that we saw our first supermarket since Helsinki—an event of such importance that Peter took a picture of it. In Poznan, itself, western style advertising was everywhere. There were good restaurants, a number of excellent bike shops, available housing (as opposed to the five-20-year waiting periods in Poland's former days) and it had all the other usual signs of a free and relatively cosmopolitan city. I had been in Poznan several years earlier on business—before the Berlin Wall came down—and the difference was startling. So was the difference in Pawel, a friend who happened to live in Poznan. I'd met him in the U.S. on business when he was a struggling, would-be entrepreneur. When he got news of the World Ride he hunted me up when I got to Poznan, and arrived in a Mercedes. He seems to have done very well for himself!

I reached Poznan by train rather than by bike. I had broken a second spoke several miles outside the city and the damage was bad enough to force me to finish the leg on the rails—a change of plans which turned out to be a good boost for the World Ride. At the train station, we were met by Peter, a Poznan Jaycee member, and we got to talking about publicity. As we talked, Peter and Jeff bicycled up to the station and the manager of the Poznan TV station happened to show up and Peter asked him if he'd do a story on the World Ride. The manager agreed, and the next thing we knew we were interviewed and filmed and the World Ride was suddenly big news in Poznan!

After our short stay there, we ended up the Polish portion of the World Ride in a very elegant, upscale Italian ice cream parlor on the last leg to the German border. There were three or four 15- or 16-year old Polish girls in the place who obviously had been drinking. They liked Americans, as most Poles do, and they introduced themselves and we talked about the music playing on the store's loudspeaker. I asked the manager if she had a Michael Jackson record and the girls went bananas, screaming so loud at the mention of that name that Peter, who was outside, probably thought we were murdering them. The whole scene was both amusing and sad. Despite the differences between Poland and the other eastern countries we'd traveled through, they had one thing in common: alcohol consumption. We came to call the countries between Finland and Germany the "Bottle Belt."

A 360-Degree Turn

When I visited Poland five or six years earlier, I had crossed the border by train into what was then East Germany. The border crossing was manned by heavily armed men with dogs. The guards came through the train and looked under the seats, inspected the baggage racks, leaving no corner unexamined, treating passengers as if they were escaped convicts. At the time I was not at all sure that one of the guards might not just take a disliking to me for some petty reason and detain me in a communist prison for god knows how long. That wasn't paranoia on my part, it was the feeling everyone got at the border crossings in those days.

Things were entirely different when I crossed the border with the World Ride team. The Polish guard passed us through without hesitation and the German guard would have done the same had we not been headed for an autobahn—one of the super high-speed German thruways where cars cruise at 100-125 mph. There was no way he would allow our bikes on that race track and we had to go back into Poland for about three miles and take another route across the border. Again, we were passed through right away.

Arriving in Germany

Crossing into Germany and getting back to the West, of course, also meant getting back to western prices. Our budget had been adequate to take care of food, lodging and other expenses in Poland and the Baltics, but now we would again be dependent on Jaycee hospitality and on whatever support they or others might give as we continued our tour.

Wolf was our World Ride Project Manager in Germany. He operated out of Berlin, and I'd been unable to reach him by phone from the Baltics or Poland, or even on my first try in former East Germany. Easy communication with more privileged western countries was one thing the secretive communist regimes had feared with a passion, and East Germany was no exception. Although it was now part of Germany proper, modern communications facilities had to be constructed from ground zero and there was still a long way to go.

On my second try, I managed to connect with Wolf and he was relieved to hear from me. He and Martin, the Junior Chamber President in Berlin, had no direct report from us on our progress, and they had tried to reach the World Ride headquarters in the U.S. several times, but they got no answer. Our headquarters was staffed by volunteer personnel rather than a paid staff and their presence wasn't predictable—which caused many problems when I needed to make such contact. I apologized to Wolf and Martin.

Berlin—Nancy!

At last, four luxurious days of not riding, more great hosting by Jaycees and, most of all, soul-warming togetherness with Nancy!

She rented a car, and after our stay in Berlin she accompanied the World Ride team on our route through Germany, using the car as our support vehicle. After having survived my ride through the Baltic States and making it to Berlin in one piece, and on time—and not having seen Nancy for about two-and-a-half months, but thinking about her constantly—you can imagine what a tremendous treat it was to look up from my bike and actually see her. And at the end of the day, when the riding was over, it was not to be an evening with Jeff and Peter, but with the woman I loved and missed so deeply! A whole week of it!

Beyond Berlin, our German route took us over the bridge at Potsdam where the Allies had exchanged prisoners with the Germans in World War II. Potsdam was also the site of the Potsdam Conference, where Allied leaders, including President Harry Truman, had met in July, 1945, to settle the question of German reparations to Russia. The Potsdam Chamber of Commerce presented us with a substantial check for the World Ride, and throughout this warm welcome and our quick tour of Potsdam's historical sites, I couldn't help but be humbled by the events which had occurred here—events which had made it possible for two Americans and a Canadian to casually ride bikes over ground where entire armies had met and fought less than 50 years earlier.

Cobblestone roads were common in German towns, causing many problems with the bikes, and we were frequently in need of repairs and adjustments—services that were now available almost everywhere. George, a bike-shop owner in Magdeburg, was particularly efficient and helpful. He was a Jehovah's Witness and had been imprisoned by the communist regime at age 21 for nearly two years for refusing to serve in the army. He declined to serve because of his religious beliefs. During World War II, the Nazis had executed many Jehovah's Witnesses for the same reason. George generously paid for our hotel in Magdeburg that night, the hotel where the former East German president who had ordered people shot on sight if they tried to cross the Berlin Wall also had stayed. Everywhere we went in Germany, we were in the midst of such solemn reminders of former times and I often found it eerie, as I did at this hotel.

In The Middle of It All

George was also responsible for entering us in a bicycle race in Erfurt, a town about half-way through our German tour. This was no local race, it was big stuff and was covered by media crews and helicopters with cameras. About 200 top German racers gathered from every part of the country and were accompanied by support vehicles and trained pit crews. Their fancy bikes were set up in finely tuned Tour de France fashion. Racing uniforms were slick and brightly colored. Many of the bikers had shaved and greased their legs for better speed and faster healing of any road rash resulting from a crash. Intricate clocking devices had been set up—this was serious business!

There we were, signed up to race, and we joined the

pack for the preliminary warm-up ride. After a few miles, and as graciously as possible, we made our way to the shoulder and let these guys go to it all by themselves. Out of 200 riders there is no doubt whatsoever that we would have come in 198th, 199th and 200th.

Somewhere west of Erfurt we celebrated Jeff's birthday. Nancy, Jeff and I ended up going to a sauna (Peter had begged off) accompanied by Helmut (a Jaycee) and his wife. We were expected to take off all our clothes and go into this communal room filled with a lot of other naked people. Nancy and I couldn't quite hack it, so we walked in covered by towels, and instantly were the odd couple and the center of attention. One guy came up to us and said, "Where the hell are you from?" So I told him, and he laughed, and then wandered off with all his glories showing. Maybe it's my conservative nature, but I think it will be a long while before I can accommodate myself to that particular European culture. Call me square.

Not So Invincible

Stalwart Peter had been lagging behind us in western Germany—very unusual—and what was even more strange was that he had been misreading the map. Peter was our map-keeper. His military experience and sense of direction were a valued asset to the World Ride, and when we questioned him about some obviously erroneous directions he'd given us, he was annoyed.

It seemed that he had the flu or something else similarly

disabling. He was disoriented, losing strength, and at one point he'd even started throwing up. Nancy took him in the car to the American military hospital in Frankfurt where he was treated and told that it was nothing serious, but that he'd have to take it easy for a few days. We took a day off, and after a good night and day's rest, Peter felt strong enough to rejoin the ride—biking easy at first and then gradually regaining his old pep over the next week or so.

We were concerned that Peter's illness was the result of tick bites in the Baltics—a really dangerous business which we'd been warned about before starting the World Ride. He'd dug a couple of ticks out of his skin—I think it was in Lithuania— but doctors in Frankfurt said that such an infection would have been marked by a bull's-eye around the entry point. He had no such mark and, thankfully, he soon recovered.

Nancy gained a new awareness of the ordeals we faced on the World Ride. She witnessed the rain and cold, and the breakdowns and the hard riding, and she'd gotten a first-hand look at our daily worries about accommodations, food and repair facilities, to say nothing of our health concerns—which were underscored by Peter's illness. She experienced the extraordinary demands placed on us by tight schedules, meetings and press interviews and she also came to appreciate, close up, how all of the above was additionally complicated by my incessant need to attend to administrative chores.

Her new understanding brought us closer. After her week was up and she flew back, I missed her terribly, but I never again had the feeling of being completely cut off from her. Lonely, yes, but no longer alone.

Our last leg out of Germany was through the Rhineland country (where the town of Trabach was—the birthplace of my family name). The rain continued, living up to its 80-percent-of-the-time average and the weather was turning colder. We were looking forward to completing the next legs through Luxembourg and Belgium to Paris. From there, we'd begin angling south to the warmer climates of Spain and North Africa.

Eleven

CHAMPAGNE AND FESTIVALS

Luxembourg/Belgium/France/Spain:
September 9–October 11

You might think from the heading of this chapter that we were riding into good times in France and Spain, but the sad truth is that the weather was abominable (rain, rain and more rain). "Champagne and festivals" is just my way of emphasizing the upbeat occasions.

The champagne part occurred on our way to Reims, France, after we'd passed through the narrow southern tips of Luxembourg and Belgium (a total of about 60 miles). We were about 25 or 30 miles from Reims, riding in evening darkness on a busy highway. Just before we were about to pull off and make camp, a couple of cars came alongside and honked us over to the side of the road. The cars were filled with a contingent of Reims Jaycees laden down with bottles of champagne, which they quickly uncorked, and an impromptu party got underway along the roadside. The whole episode was French to the core—spontaneous, high-spirited and thoroughly delightful. A great little party!

The whole French portion of the trip, in fact—despite the combined miseries of rain, traffic and truly terrible riding conditions—was more than made-up for by the high spirits and entertaining welcomes of the French Jaycees and their friends. In Paris, for example, Francoise, a woman I'd just been introduced to, let me crash in her apartment for the night. I'm a big guy (6'6"), a total stranger, and I was weathered, weary and by no means sparkling clean, yet she didn't give it a second thought. Before I retired, we sat around playing a Cat Stevens CD— not a bad way for a tired wanderer to end the day in a strange country.

Although we took a day off in Paris, my Jaycee business and other administrative duties only allowed me time for a four-hour tour of the city—which is not nearly enough to see it all—but the rain was so constant and miserable that there wasn't much point in it anyway. I heard Parisiens complaining about the weather, but at least they didn't have to face it on bikes on truck-filled highways! Jeff jokingly renamed our mission the "World Ride Against Rain." He developed a rash from the constant wetness (one eye nearly being swollen shut for a time), but his and Peter's consistent good humor about our trials and tribulations saved this from being the World Ride's low-point for morale. The same weather was to continue not only through France, but also on most of our ride through "sunny" Spain.

Somewhere south of Paris, we decided to cancel our Algerian portion of the ride—saving nine days and avoiding what had now become a truly dangerous part of the world. According to news reports, Algeria was literally at war with itself. Reporters told of visitors being shot by revolutionary groups, several countries had officially warned their citizens not to travel to Algeria and a government dawn-to-dusk curfew had been instituted. We didn't need to take a vote to decide on skipping that part of our route.

Time for a French Toast

By the time we reached Bergerac in southern France, the swelling around Jeff's eyes had subsided somewhat, but the rash had persisted, and the Bergerac Jaycees arranged for some free medical help. We received lessons in wine appreciation, and listened carefully as they proudly explained differences in variety and nomenclature, thus increasing our knowledge (mine, at least) from zero to maybe a one or two. It was here that I also had to face a main entree of something described to me as pig stomach. It was touted as a delicacy, the French euphemism for stuff that usually appears in American cat food.

Peter's fluent French entitled him to be spokesman for the World Ride while we were in France and he generally handled the press interviews while I sat back and enjoyed a rest. Most French journalists spoke English, but French was the language of choice and Peter served the World Ride's cause with honors. We were public relations pros—when the journalists got their cameras out we knew just how to group together and align our bikes and assume the stances the photographers wanted.

Another thing we'd become adept at was spending down

our loose change just before border crossings. We could exchange our folding money from one country to the next, but not coins. So we'd stuff ourselves with food just before entering a new country and ride the next few miles down the road in near slumber. (I learned to buy canned food and store it in my bike bags.)

South of Bergerac we were met by Yves, a Jaycee from Agen, who escorted us to his house for the night—a stunning 13th-Century chateau. His wife, Danielle, served us crab meat (heated in the crab shell) and rice, and then we retired to our rooms and exquisite furnishings and slept 11 hours in luxury beyond my descriptive abilities. Jeff's gears were slipping badly and there was no way we could get them repaired and make it the 80 miles to Toulouse the next day. So, reluctantly, and with downcast faces, we allowed ourselves to be talked into another day and night at the Chateau. It was just one of the many great sacrifices we had to make for the World Ride cause.

Jeff had his Visa credit card swallowed by an automatic teller machine in Toulouse—an occurrence of potentially dire consequence. But the Jaycees came to the rescue, vouching for Jeff with the bank management and arranging for him to get his card back. Moral: Before you go to Europe, or maybe anywhere at all, join the Jaycees!

After Toulouse, we made a six-mile climb up the foothills of the Pyrenees—the mountain range bordering Spain—and toured the magnificent, perfectly preserved medieval French city of Carcassonne. We camped on the city's outskirts for the night and then headed for

Perpignan, our last stop in France. We literally hadn't had dry clothes in two weeks—even our bike bags smelled—and this last day in France was to be no exception. The downpours, accompanied by thunder storms, were incredible in the foothills, and whenever we rode down from a peak it was a quantum leap in body-soaking, not to mention our lightning-rod potential in that excessively high country.

Just over the next ridges, however, lay Spain and the Mediterranean, and we all surmised that things would surely get better. Not a chance.

The Rain in Spain

Cold rain escorted us right into Gerona—but the Jaycees warmed us up with an enthusiastic welcome and press conference, followed by some happy socializing afterward (lots of pretty women) which was especially warming to Jeff and Peter. I was so smitten with Nancy that I couldn't have even looked at another woman. But Jeff and Peter were fancy-free and tailor-made for a country like Spain where festivals and social gatherings always seemed to be in progress. Jeff walked over to me and jokingly threatened to abandon the World Ride: "Richard, you're on your own. You think we're kidding, we're not." Imagine that? I mean why would two young men prefer to hang around with beautiful women in a social hall rather than ride bikes in that challenging European weather and change flats and fix spokes and worry about instant death in traffic?

Spain was the land of flat tires. We had about a dozen among us (three in one day) on the way down the Mediterranean coast. Our particular route at this time was on one of Spain's national highways—sounds impressive—but a rough road surface and constant debris (such as broken glass) were real tire-busters. All of these flats occurred in continuing cold rain, of course, and if riding through the weather was miserable, kneeling down to fix tire after tire was worse.

On the way to Sabadell, the rain had let up a bit and we passed a lady who was all dressed up standing along the roadside. A couple of hills further on, we passed another. And then another. We were told later that they were prostitutes and that their beckoning glances were common along this stretch of road.

Ramone was our World Ride Project Manager for Spain. We met up with him in Sabadell and he graciously agreed to fax the Junior Chamber International and European Jaycees with the news that we had made it safely into Spain. He and his wife treated us to a sensational Spanish dinner. Dinner time in Spain is traditionally at 10 p.m., lunch at 4 p.m. and siesta between 1:30 and 4 p.m.—siesta being the time during which nobody in Spain does anything if they can help it. You can imagine what havoc these customs would have played with our riding schedule if we'd followed them! Ramone told us of a big festival in progress at Tarragona, our next scheduled stop, and we headed out bright and early the next morning. Before we got there (a matter of 50 short miles) I had two more flat tires.

It may seem that the only thing Spaniards do is hang out at festivals, but that is not the case—the Spanish Jaycees had things organized efficiently. Meetings and press conferences were everything we could have wished for, and despite the weather and the roads and casual customs, the Jaycees saw to it that the World Ride accomplished its mission in Spain. These people truly loved life and it was a pleasure to see, and they got things done while enjoying it all. How they do it, I can't imagine. It can take an hour or more to get served at a restaurant (Peter once went for a long sight-seeing walk after placing his order), and this sort of relaxed ambiance is typical. It's what one does in Spain—one relaxes and enjoys life. It's not every place where you can go into a strange town and see 30 guys standing on each others' shoulders in the town square building a body pyramid.

Costumes, firecrackers, explosions, music, dancing, water dunkings (I was a victim)—it's all part of the festivals and good times. Now and then the weather would break for a few hours, the sun would come out, and the Spain of travel folders would emerge in all its glory. On one such day, Jeff rode along shirtless, singing away merrily, a thoroughly happy man—he said it reminded him of Tucson. Such moments were all too few for us, I'm afraid. Let's face it, the almost constant rain was an abnormality. We were riding through semi-arid land where it supposedly rained only 20 percent of the time! We just hit it wrong. We got the full 20 percent.

And Then There Was The Dog

Wildlife in Spain is interesting. We saw a gang of rats along the roadside, each one as big as a cat. We shuddered and stayed well clear of their territory. Potato bugs—the slimy little creatures one finds in rotten logs—crawled into my sleeping bag one night when Jeff had persuaded us to sleep in a field without tent cover. They woke me up by crawling on my neck. Half asleep, and in total darkness, I didn't know what they were, and throughout the night they continued to wake me up sporadically and I'd pick them off my legs and throw them aside. Morning light showed me what I'd been dealing with.

We were just finishing a climb up a hill (when we were at our slowest and most vulnerable) when I heard Peter yell, "Go! Go! Go!" Peter was at the rear of the team and I slowed down and turned around to see what he was so excited about. When I turned around, I saw a dog. He'd come out from a driveway at a dead run, lips pulled back, snarling and salivating at the thought of some good bike-rider flesh. This was no bluff—the dog meant it—and Peter had seen all this from the rear and yelled like crazy. Luckily, the dog lost his footing on the slippery pavement in his enthusiasm, taking a moment to regain his legs, and we were able to get up to speed and deny him his lunch.

Apart from the nightmarish roads (I'm talking about maintenance and conditions, not wildlife), there are definitely some negative sides to Spain. Medical service, for example, is free, but it can be slower than in other countries we visited. The Jaycees told us of a sick woman who had to wait two months to even be examined. Medically, Spain is far from being a paradise, but free is free and that's quite something when compared to other countries like the United States which offers very expensive medical services. Spain may not be a perfect society, but there is an appealing spirit that makes one want to come back and spend more time. Many large communities of young American and European expatriots bear witness to that appeal.

On to North Africa

Head winds were fierce as we reached the southernmost parts of Spain, prompting Jeff to suggest that we should ride around the world the other way if we tried this again. Some major problems had cropped up on Jeff's bike, and as we neared Gibraltar, close to our ferry point to North Africa, we became seriously concerned about getting repairs and parts before crossing. We were coming down to the line, now, and our thoughts were starting to focus on the serious business of traveling through unknown and unpredictable territory.

One major dilemma was how to avoid biking in Algeria. We'd be starting the North African portion of the World Ride in Morocco. Our next destination was Tunisia. Algeria lay between the two. So we either had to go through Algeria on a train or over it in a plane. We learned that the plane fare was $270 each—far more than any of us could afford. A train ride would be a lot cheaper, but it would require Algerian transit visas. With all the unrest in that country we might or might not get such visas, and we also didn't think a train ride would assure our safety. It was a real dilemma and we did what any responsible, decisive thinkers would do—we put it off, hoping to figure it all out when we reached Morocco.

There were some first-class bike shops on the way to Gibraltar, and Jeff's immediate bike problems were solved. Peter had bike problems, too, but they were minor in comparison and taken care of quickly. About this time, Jeff managed to fall off his bike in a rainstorm. He was considerably scraped up, requiring antiseptic gauze pads, which we had with us. It could have been far more serious, and it dramatically reminded us of the medical uncertainties we'd be facing in North Africa. We'd been exceptionally fortunate up to now—nearly six thousand miles of biking to date, and except for a couple of bouts with flu and a few cuts, scrapes, rashes, stiff necks and a sore back here and there, we'd come through in fine form. So far, no complaints, and we fervently hoped it would stay that way.

Gibraltar hadn't been our first choice for a port of embarkation to Morocco; we'd been hoping to ferry over sooner from other towns up the line. But I was trying to arrange a discount for the World Ride team, and when I couldn't get it in one place we rode on to the next place, and so on. No luck at all, and we eventually ended up close to Gibraltar.

I had a tough time trying to reach Nancy during these

last legs in Spain. I kept leaving messages, asking her to call me at our various hotels and campgrounds, hoping the manager would rouse me if her call came in. I heard the phone ring in a couple of these places, but nobody came for me. I suspected it really was Nancy calling, but the managers just didn't bother to tell me—maybe they'd never been in love. Late one night, the lady manager at a campground near the Rock of Gibraltar did come for me— rushing out and shaking my tent, shouting at me to get up and get to the phone. At last! I could not have imagined going off to North Africa without speaking to Nancy! She told me she'd made arrangements to meet me in Hong Kong, less than two months away, and that thought alone would help me overcome any conceivable problems that lay ahead.

It was decided that we'd take the ferry to Ceuta (a Spanish enclave in Morocco) rather than Tangier—no charge for our bikes if we went to Ceuta. So, this we did, biking through Ceuta after our ferry ride and then crossing the border into Morocco. The border guards were pleasant, wishing us a good trip, and one of them asked if this was our first visit to Morocco. I said, "Yes." Peter said, "Yes." But Jeff said, "No, I was born here." And he had indeed been born in Morocco—his father had been in the American military and the family was stationed there.

By the time we'd biked a few miles into Morocco, we knew we'd entered an entirely new world. It was like nothing I had ever seen.

Twelve

STRANGE PLACES

Morocco/Tunisia:
October 11–22

Morocco is a land of immense heat and high winds. Narrow roads without shoulders cross a generally sandy, arid landscape which, at times, is as flat as a board and at other times rises and falls sharply into steep, hilly terrain. We shared these roads with mule-drawn carts and Mercedes taxis. The latter were invariably green, driven recklessly and crammed with an inconceivable number of passengers, all of them shouting and waving their arms at us as they wildly sped by, the driver honking us out of the way.

Beggars and hustlers frequently approached us, asking for money or offering services and deals. It was threatening and uncomfortable and we stayed together at all times, trying to look as formidable as possible.

The towns were mostly shanties with open-air stalls that smelled awful; it was a general stench we couldn't quite pin down, but it was always present. Women wore full-length gowns and head-coverings, avoiding eye contact, while men congregated together as if they were a different species. Oddly enough, however, there was an air of festivity and gaiety about the towns; the people were happy and enjoying themselves.

On many occasions, I had the feeling the World Ride team was providing a town's entertainment for the day. People were astounded at us; kids would run out from their yards and wave at us as we rode by; men would point and then talk among themselves and then point some more.

We encountered a surprising number of police along the road. They'd often stop us, but we were obviously non-threatening and they'd smile and let us proceed. Jeff usually got around to telling these police that he was born in Morocco and it seemed to help. Anyway, we never had a problem.

Traffic police carry strings with a cluster of spikes attached at the end, odd-looking contraptions which they throw into the road if they suspect an oncoming car isn't going to stop. The police have another delightful habit in Morocco—some of them anyway. We were told by a Canadian couple that drug dealers occasionally work hand-in-hand with the police in the following scam: The drug dealer spots a Westerner at a restaurant, for example, places a bag of chocolate-looking hashish on the Westerner's table and then walks off. The unsuspecting diner picks up the "chocolate" and is immediately confronted by a policeman for having drugs in his possession. The only way to avoid severe trouble is to pay-off the policeman, who in turn splits the take with the drug dealer. Nifty, isn't it?

Who'll Stop the Rain?

Our first destination in Morocco was Tangier, just a few miles down the road. As hot and dry as it was when the sun occasionally came out, you may be sure we brought the rain with us and experienced our usual complement of downpours and chills. We even had to pull into a hotel the first night on the road to dry out. And when I say we'd brought the rain, I mean just that. Tangier was in the midst of a drought of such severity that every night for the past three years the city's water had been turned off from about 6 p.m. to 6 a.m. The World Ride team arrived and bingo! It started to rain!

As soon as we reached Tangier, I phoned our local contact and was told quite bluntly that he could not arrange accommodations for us on such short notice. We'd tried several times to reach him from France and Spain without success. Whether he expected us or not, I was shocked at his cold reception. A day later, the contact failed to keep an appointment with me and his credibility plummeted to rock-bottom. Up to that point on our World Ride adventure, such a thing was a most unusual experience. In another week or so, however, we were to have another one just like it in Italy.

Visa Woes

From information we picked up from casual conversations with Moroccans, we were finally persuaded that the only way to avoid biking in Algeria was to book passage on a train through that country directly to Tunisia. We would still need Algerian travel visas, however, and this meant going to the Algerian Consulate in Rabat, the capital of Morocco. We could have bicycled the 250 miles or so to Rabat and seen more of Morocco, but our bikes needed repairs and adjustments and we decided to save time for those necessities by taking a train. The cost was $8 each and 75¢ for each bike. The trip to Rabat went smoothly, except at the end, when we went to the baggage area to retrieve our bikes and were told by the baggage handler that he had sold them! It was his idea of a little joke and he was amused at our signs of cardiac arrest.

Later that day, when we were filling out our visa applications, we discovered that Thursdays and Fridays (the next two days) were weekends in Algeria and that processing would be delayed. We weren't given any promises of success with the visa applications and we were told conflicting stories about the Algerian situation. We ended up discouraged, worried and still unsure of anything having to do with Algeria. It was the most serious situation we'd faced on the World Ride to date and we solemnly discussed it over a late afternoon lunch of pastry and tea. It was after this lunch that Lady Luck suddenly made her appearance on behalf of the World Ride team.

Lady Luck in Morocco

Peter had not yet acquired his visa for Bangladesh, (one of the countries on our itinerary), and having some time on our hands, we accompanied him to the Bangladesh Embassy where we met Ms. Luck in the person of Jameilla. She was a staff member at the Embassy, Moroccan by birth and married to a U.S. Marine. While Peter was filling out his Bangladesh visa application, Jeff and I started talking with her and she was fascinated by the World Ride and its objectives. She was a lovely woman—bright, articulate and representative of the truer Moroccan culture away from the highways. We explained our Algerian problems, and she directed us to a travel agency whose director might be counted on to have sympathy with our cause and give us a discount on plane tickets directly to Tunisia—such a trip required no Algerian travel visas.

I thanked her and soon after we went to the travel agency (Africvoyages), telling the director about our situation, and he was indeed sympathetic and supportive of our World Ride Against Cancer and offered us plane tickets from Casablanca to Tunis at 50 percent off—just like that! And you may be sure I thanked him profusely—and just as profusely again thanked Jameilla.

In addition to that greatest of help, Jameilla also used Embassy time and Embassy phone lines to arrange publicity for the World Ride in L'Opinion, one of Morocco's large newspapers with a substantial international circulation throughout North Africa and Europe. Even then Jameilla wasn't finished. After she left work that day, she introduced us to her friend, Rashine, and they drove us to an art exhibit and gave us a quick tour of the city during which she explained that Morocco had been the very first of all countries to recognize American independence.

The following day, Jameilla took us to a diplomatic function, the purpose of which was a pleasant surprise—to raise funds for a local cancer organization. It was a grand occasion—among those in attendance were the three princesses of the king, soldiers in dress uniforms, finely tailored diplomats, Moroccan royalty, elegantly-dressed ladies and the World Ride team in T-shirts. We enjoyed a great afternoon and evening graciously provided by a new friend who took us under her wing and gave us a different and better view of Moroccans.

On The Road to Casablanca

When we left on the train for Casablanca the next day, it wasn't easy to say good-bye to Jameilla. I gave her the World Ride office address in the U.S. since she and her husband were expecting to go there shortly. I sincerely hope I have the opportunity to repay the kindness she so generously showered on us in Rabat.

Casablanca was a city I very much wanted to tour but, as usual on the ride, we had no time for it. As Jeff (or Peter) said, ours was a "World Ride Sampler." After reaching

Casablanca, we rode to the airport in the dark, slept on the terminal floor, were patted down by guards and finally ushered onto the plane for Tunis in the morning. I had moments of guilt about avoiding a bike ride through Algeria—maybe we all did—but it was a rational decision based on the country's turmoil and the excessive dislike of Westerners among some of the revolutionary parties. They were killing Western tourists, and I couldn't imagine a more tempting target than three unescorted bicycle riders.

Tunis was our only destination in Tunisia, our entire route in that country involving no more than a six-mile leg, including the ride from the airport to the city. But it was a memorable visit nonetheless.

Exchange Madness

To begin with, we abruptly discovered that Tunisian monetary law disallowed the exchange of our Moroccan money into Tunisian dinars. This may have applied only to tourists—I don't know. We had about $180 (U.S.) in Moroccan bills, a substantial sum, but the personnel at the several exchange counters at the airport wouldn't touch it. Some of them even laughed at our stupidity in asking.

I was more angry about this than with anything else that happened on our crusade—mad beyond words, with no ifs, ands or buts, and absolutely determined to get our money exchanged. We mounted our bikes and rode to Tunis, going directly to the Junior Chamber office. Our ring was answered by a beautiful, English-speaking Tunisian woman who promptly called the Junior Chamber President who was out of the office, but who told the woman he'd call the International Vice President to help us. Would we please call back in about an hour-and-a-half?

The woman was pleasant and efficient and I had the feeling from the president's concern and response that we were back in the friendly arms of Jaycees. But I was still seething and not willing to wait another 90 minutes, and decided to go into a nearby bank and get our money exchanged. After going through a couple of lower-echelon people who repeatedly told me "No!" I finally reached an executive who stood still long enough for me to demonstrate the necessity of an exchange. I did this by showing him the World Ride article in L'Opinion. The article clearly explained our charitable mission and the extent of our travels and everywhere indicated that we were hardly on a rich-man's tour. Instead, it pointed out clearly that we were self-supporting and dependent upon help and good will in the countries we visited. An understanding grin eventually crossed his face and he said he'd be going to Morocco in the next couple of weeks and he'd do me a favor and personally exchange my money. His name was Aimar. When I returned with the Tunisian money, Peter and Jeff were blown away.

The Jaycees Come Through Again

From the looks of Tunis, it seemed like a repeat of Tangier and Rabat. Arafat, the leader of the Palestinian

Liberation Organization, was rumored to have a home here and we expected to see signs of the PLO and other military doings, but we saw nothing of such things. What we did experience, however, was the enthusiasm and support of the Tunisian Jaycees.

Karim was the Jaycee who was sent by the Junior Chamber President to watch over us, and his first act was to let us throw our sleeping bags on the floor of the Jaycee office and call it home—no hotel expenses! He then took us to dinner (I had eggs and tortilla chips) where we were entertained by a very talented blind pianist. Karim was 32 and the Junior Chamber was his whole life. He dedicated himself to it fully, loved every aspect of it, spoke impeccable English and enjoyed getting things done. He arranged an important press conference for us the following morning, got us malaria pills for southeast Asia—at a cost of $1.50 per 100 pills versus the one dollar per pill Jeff had paid back in the U.S.—and he generally took over stewardship of the World Ride project in Tunis.

The only unfortunate incident in Tunis was the loss of Peter's camera. He'd put it in the bottom of his laundry bag at the Jaycee office and then left the office for no more than five minutes. When he returned, the bag was gone. The Jaycees helped us look everywhere, figuring out every possibility, but the bottom line was that the bag and camera had been stolen, most probably by a non-Jaycee person on one of the upper floors who had noted our comings and goings. The Jaycees were mortified, as upset as Peter; they considered it a personal violation. For

Peter, of course, on his tight budget, it was a serious loss. We were all sorry.

Making Things Happen

Karim really outdid himself for the World Ride team in helping to arrange free passage for us on the ferry from Tunis to Genoa, Italy—first class, no less, and all meals included! We met with the director of the CTN Ferry Company to show our gratitude, and he said he was impressed with the World Ride and its worthy cause and was delighted to help.

As a final act of support and kindness to us, Karim arranged for the exchange of our Tunisian dinar into Italian lira—a truly outstanding Jaycee and the best of goodwill ambassadors for his country!

The World Ride team at the Massachusetts border a few days before the end of the World Ride. From the start, finishing safely was always on our minds.

GARY J. H. WONG

The World Ride team in Poitiers, France. Kneeling from left: Jeff, Peter and Richard.

Peter fixes a flat on the road to
Casablanca, Morocco.

A corner of the
killing wall at the
Nazi death camp
in Kaunas,
Lithuania.

A Japanese
welcome sign
for the World
Ride team,
"Just call me
Mister."

Richard and girlfriend Nancy in Germany.

The World Ride team with new friends near Tokyo, Japan.

A day in the life in Nepal.

The Jaycees World Ride Against Cancer check presentation to The Jimmy Fund of Dana-Farber Cancer Institute (November, 1994). Pictured left to right: John Stamper, Diane Barow, Richard Drorbaugh, Jane D'Arcy, Jim Calder and Mary Canigiani.

116

Thirteen

THE LAST OF EUROPE

Italy/Greece:
October 23–November 4

Genoa was our ferry destination in Italy. From there, we took the train to Pisa on Italy's west coast to start the Italian leg from west to east. This would be about 250 miles to Ancona on the Adriatic Sea. At Ancona, we would take another ferry (the last major ferry trip of the World Ride) to Patras, Greece. From Patras, we would bike 140 miles to Athens, our last stop in Europe, and then fly to India.

Italy, I'm sorry to say, is largely memorable for the problems we encountered, not only with my bike and with the lingering illness I'd contracted from the Moroccan rain, but also with the people we met (and didn't meet). It was the luck of our particular trip—we just ran into an isolated string of unpleasant events. It can happen to anyone, in any country, at any time—as experienced travelers will attest. The time and place for us was to be Italy. Aside from the stunning beauty of the Italian landscape and the cultural magnificence of Florence, there is precious little I can report with a positive ring.

Floundering in Florence

Our contact in Florence left us to flounder. In fairness to him, Florence had not been on our original itinerary and he was first notified of our route through a telephone message I left for him soon after our ferry landing in Genoa. Our original itinerary had been to ferry from Tunis to Sicily and then bike across southern Italy. But our budget and common sense wouldn't allow us to refuse the free ferry passage to Genoa, and thus we began our Italian portion of the World Ride in northern Italy.

I wasn't able to reach our Florence contact on the telephone until 8 p.m. the day we arrived. I had been forced to leave messages on three previous calls. Firm arrangements were made to meet the next morning and we dearly needed his help. We were in a Florence hotel, which we couldn't afford, and we'd had a series of bike problems that had dragged our budgets down considerably.

Our contact didn't show for the morning appointment. After another call to his office, which was unsuccessful, and waiting around for an inordinate amount of time we decided not to waste any more of it and headed out of town.

Right away, we had more bike problems, serious enough to cause us to return to Florence and stay another night. Again I called the contact, leaving messages at his office, and again he made no effort to get back to me throughout that day and night. He'd blown us off a second time. Considering the state of our finances, the condition of our bikes and our increasingly low spirits, the entire episode was worse than our experience in Morocco.

Bad Tempers Abound

Our Italian route, at least from Pisa to Ancona (which was most of it), was marked by constant equipment breakdowns or near breakdowns—spokes, tires, sprockets, chains—and we spent many hours in various bike shops getting an earful of Italian slang and swear words and bad tempers. In one bike shop, where I had to use the rest room, a couple of employees banged on the door impatiently. When I came out a guy walked up to me, swearing, and acted as if he wanted to tangle. I waited, willing to oblige him, but he just spouted off and walked away.

Italian cops, angry and belligerent, ordered us off a highway that was off-limits to bikers, knowing full well we were strangers and didn't know the rules. For a moment, I thought we were going to be hauled off to jail. I'd been understandably concerned about this sort of thing in Russia and the Baltic States and in North Africa, but we came the closest to it in Italy—one of the last places I would have expected it. We kept saying things like, "Okay, okay! Calm down! We're going. We're going! Take it easy!"

The hope of getting a discounted ferry passage to Greece—which I had asked for in the World Ride's name when we got to Ancona—came to a rude dead end real fast.

One exception to our unpleasantness in Italy was the generosity and empathy of a lone guy in a back alleyway next to a closed bike shop. I don't know whether he worked for the bike shop or was free-lancing in bike repair, but he replaced two of my broken spokes and trued (straightened) the wheel expertly. When he learned of the World Ride cause through an English-speaking Italian cyclist standing beside me he refused to charge. That was the first and only break we got in Italy.

Touching Home Base

With all the repair delays, and having no Jaycee appointments or other scheduled affairs to attend to, I caught up on a lot of administrative tasks and other World Ride business in Italy. For one thing, I reversed a phone call to Billy Costa at KISS 108 FM in Boston, a popular radio host who was keeping track of the World Ride progress. He hadn't heard from me for a while and he gladly accepted the call and recorded 10 to 15 minutes of my World Ride updates.

I also sent off the latest portion of my film documentary of the World Ride to Russ Dougherty and Dave Sinclair of Video Excellence in Swansea, Mass. These were friends of mine in the U.S. who would combine this tape with others they'd received earlier and edit them down to a 10–to 15–minute presentation I was to make at the 1993 Junior Chamber International Congress in November in Hong Kong. Nancy planned on attending, and would bring the finished presentation tape with her. Being sure the World Ride team reached Hong Kong in time for the Congress had dictated many decisions I'd made about our biking schedule. In Italy, it was already the last week in October, and you can imagine my concern about making it to Hong Kong with only a month to go.

Nancy, and this seems a good place to bring it in, was really my representative in the U.S. Our phone conversations were largely composed of lists of things I needed her to do for the World Ride, and despite her very busy schedule, she always managed to get them done. She apprised me of our publicity in the States, relevant developments affecting the Jaycees and the World Ride organization and generally kept her eye on things—an immense help.

Her only complaint was that we had no time to discuss our personal affairs. It was always World Ride business rather than Nancy and Richard business and I wholly agreed with her. I often felt that I was being insensitive to unreel my list of things to be attended to. Heaven knows, I adored and missed her and wanted to talk about us as much as she did, but time and money wouldn't allow it and we both knew it. Not always patient, but generally good-humored, she accepted this unusual situation. She is my incredible good fortune.

Arrivederci, Italy!

We wrapped up our Italian route with a cold ride over a steep mountain range where temperatures were near freezing. Then we swept down into Ancona where we caught the ferry for Patras, Greece.

Greece was the country I had looked forward to with the

greatest amount of anticipation, but traveler's luck had ordained that this was not to be the right time. At another point in time it probably would have been glorious.

We landed in Patras on October 31 with a 140-mile ride ahead of us to Athens and managed to cover about half of it before the day ended. We were biking on a major highway and we made sure it was legal; all of us were very shaky after our experience in Italy. Everything was cool here—smiling cops and toll-takers (no toll for bikes) and a general atmosphere of friendliness—a welcome change.

Often we'd meet up with other cyclists, either solo or in groups, and it was no exception on this highway in Greece where we fell in with three cyclists who had biked down from Amsterdam. Two were from Canada and one was from Denmark and we swapped stories about bike failures, budgets, currency exchanges. We thoroughly enjoyed their amazement at our having covered more than 20 countries, totaling 6,000 miles—and that we had nearly 8,000 still to go. They'd been complimenting themselves on having traversed 1,000 miles and they were stunned by our figures.

They were an easy-going bunch—humorous, knowledgeable—and we would have made a very compatible six-man team. It was with some reluctance that we eventually rode on ahead, having to part company with them to adhere to our tight schedule. We didn't say good-bye, however, until we'd given them the phone number of Anna, our contact at Junior Chamber Greece's office in Athens, in case they ran into problems.

I'd tried to reach Anna a couple of times earlier without

success, but I managed to make phone contact just after our fellow bikers left. It turned out she had the flu and wouldn't be able to meet us on the road the next day outside of Athens. She had tentatively planned press conferences and other publicity for us, including a meeting with the mayor, but she had been forced to hold things in reserve because she hadn't heard from us and couldn't set firm appointments. She had even called Italy to locate us and confirm our schedule, but no word about her inquiry, of course, was passed along to us. I had sent her an update from Tunis, which I felt was adequate, but I probably should have called her from Italy and I apologized for not having done so there. But I refused to beat myself up too badly in light of how full my hands were with other pressing problems in Italy.

Gentle and Genteel Greece

After riding about 60 miles on that first day in Greece, we camped near a beach on the Gulf of Corinthia. It was very beautiful—the soft, lovely, pastoral Greece of St. Paul's journeys. In the morning, going alone to the beach for a few moments of reflection, I saw a shabbily dressed older woman throwing a fishing-line into the water in what appeared to be an effort to catch breakfast or lunch. I watched her quietly for several minutes and was moved by it—a strange, small memory that has stayed with me.

There was nothing calm and pastoral as we neared Athens, however. Here, the highway widened out and we began to encounter heavy evening traffic even faster and wilder and more terrifying than on the "A" road in Britain. This was, in fact, as we all agreed, the second most horrendous stretch of traffic we'd encountered on the entire European ride. As Peter put it, "I saw my life passing before me."

Night had arrived, compounding our vulnerability, and I was both petrified and angry. So angry, in fact, and so pumped up with adrenalin, that it overcame my fear and I decided to tackle the problem aggressively and bike at the fastest speed possible to get us out of the death-trap. I immediately took the lead, and the World Ride team went into a flat-out dash for Anna's place, even passing some slower traffic here and there. Anna, despite her flu, and having previously doubted she'd be able to meet us on the outskirts of Athens, had nevertheless arranged for a friend to drive her and they accompanied us on this mad sprint to her home. When we got there, she and a girlfriend offered us pizza and baklava, and although we couldn't eat much of it because we were so wound up, we were eternally grateful to be alive for the opportunity.

Dedication Personified

Anna was the personification of Jaycee dedication. She had arranged some student housing for us, which saved us a bundle during our three-day stay. She also insisted that she personally pick up the hefty tab for the several overseas administrative calls I had to make. She was a mover and a shaker, constantly on the telephone for her own business as well as making arrangements for the World Ride team. She saw to it that we had what we needed, demonstrating that once again we were back in the good hands of dedicated Jaycees. She even arranged a press conference for us within sight of the Acropolis—it doesn't get more impressive than that! Aside from being interviewed by newspaper reporters, we were also filmed by a TV crew for about an hour.

I lingered a bit after it was over, taking in the grandeur of this most eminent of all hill-tops, and also talking with the AIESEC students who had graciously made room for us in their dormitories. Several of them had even come along to watch the publicity proceedings. Standing near the students was a cancer survivor, Sophia, who was accompanied by a male friend who had once toured the Dana-Farber Cancer Institute in Boston. We explained that the money raised on the World Ride was being donated to Dana-Farber and he was moved to the point of tears.

One of the newspaper reporters at our interview had attended Boston College, where Nancy had graduated, and I might mention that this sort of coincidence frequently popped up on the World Ride. On the road, on ferries and in restaurants, chance meetings with strangers often led to mutual connections, not only geographically or personally, but also in respect to the universal concern with cancer and its cure, as with Sophia and her friend. More than once, I remember impromptu conversations that were wholly devoted to cancer rather than to the usual things strangers are apt to chat about, such as the weather or common links to one place or another.

Smile for The Camera

Not content with the perfection of the press conference near the Acropolis, Anna had still another publicity meeting set up for us—a live interview at a television station in Athens. This was a first for the World Ride team, complete with facial make-up and other necessary preparations. We were accompanied to the studio by Tasos, a fellow Jaycee assigned to us by Anna, and after our interview he treated us to dinner and then took us back to his office where he offered me free phone service to the U.S. to update my friends at the American Automobile Association, a World Ride sponsor.

And so it went in Athens. We were fed, housed, publicized, bankrolled and accommodated at every turn. The word "support" doesn't begin to do justice to the efforts expended on the World Ride's behalf by Anna and the other members of the Junior Chamber in Athens. It was remarkable—a great upbeat ending to our European tour.

Fourteen

HUMAN MASSES

India: November 5–11

It was about a 10-hour flight to New Delhi, India. My seat companion was a 28-year-old German hiker on his way to Nepal and he kindly offered to purchase a World Ride T-shirt (one of the incidental ways the team raised money for cancer research). Free alcohol was served on the flight and I stashed away a couple of small bottles of rum for the team's future celebration. Country western and rock-and-roll music was standard fare from the headphones, an odd thing to listen to as I looked down on Afghanistan and Pakistan and tried to psych myself up for travels in India and Nepal.

New Delhi was our entrance into the Third World. We had thought of the Baltics and Morocco and Tunisia as being in that category, but nothing had prepared us for the real thing. There are positive and negative aspects to traveling in a real third world country. As for India, I will start with the negative because we were struck by it instantly when we landed in New Delhi.

The foremost reality was the incredible mass of humanity—crushing, inescapable hoards of people. It was totally engulfing and suffocating, no room for even the smallest personal space. To this westerner, the sheer number of people was almost incomprehensible, and it was to be the same everywhere in our Indian travels.

The Real Third World

The second, and equally incredible, was the stench that permeated the air. Sewage often ran through open troths, and black exhaust spewed from trucks and buses and from Fifties-era taxis, filling the air with intolerable smog and pollution that burned the eyes and stifled breath.

Add to this the irritation of public loudspeakers blaring forth scratchy, abrasive music as if from old phonographs. We did not want to breathe the air, drink the water or walk the streets. We just wanted out. We wanted to wake up—it was truly the stuff of nightmares.

We had no desire to go sight seeing and we left the city as quickly as possible. We headed out from the downtown area on a rough, gravelly road (the main thruway) where we were immediately enmeshed in horrific traffic composed of taxis, buses, rickshaws, bicycles, trucks, motorbikes, scooters and every other form of wheeled transportation imaginable. Women in long, white saris rode side-saddle behind their husbands on some of the motorbikes. The traffic was as jammed as the masses of pedestrians were. Cows (sacred to some Hindus) roamed at will on the sidewalks and in the road, hanging out wherever they chose and adding their own variety of stench and confusion to everything else.

We looked upon our ride out of the city as an escape, so much so that we kept riding after dark—half-blinded by headlights glaring through the pollution. The two-lane roads were worse than they'd been in New Delhi—no shoulders, but plenty of ruts and potholes—all filled with debris. Low-powered buses would try to pass each other, racing side-by-side for long distances and frequently forcing us to pull off the road.

More Human Warmth

The positive side to our Indian travels was the people—immensely polite, gentle, filled with good humor and obvious good feelings toward us. Theirs was a basic, uncomplicated life, so uncomplicated, in fact, that it was enviable. Their contentment derived from familiar things such as family and friends and a parochial environment. It was not surprising that we attracted crowds of onlookers everywhere we went. We were strange objects, we Westerners, with our fancy bikes and good health—like exotic creatures in a zoo. People would gather around us and gaze while pointing and nodding to others in the crowd. They would stand so close that we rarely had room to repair a tire or adjust a spoke. We represented a wholly alien culture to them—one of wealth and plenty and they could not conceive of it.

We decided not to camp out, realizing we would have no peace or privacy, and opted instead for a series of hotel rooms. These were almost invariably dirty and unswept with minimal toilet facilities (often just a hole). In one such room, lit by a lone bulb without a shade, lizards climbed the walls. At another hotel birds flew freely in the dining room above our table. While at the "lizard" hotel, two young men knocked on our door and wanted to talk with us to find out more about our world. The contrast between the conditions we found so deplorable and the people we found so likable was stark to say the least. We encountered such contrast everywhere we went in India.

The rural area roads were lined with rickety, match-stick telephone poles. Sanitation was as bad as it was in the cities and towns, rivers were the chief laundromats, people were thin and hollow-faced, raggedly dressed and showed signs of disease and malnutrition. And there was every-where—in the fields, along the roadside—haunting images of poverty: scarecrow women with bundles of hay on their head, naked children, cattle pulling wobbly wooden carts and vultures perched on tree limbs.

Unimaginable Poverty

We had not expected such things—not in India, not any-where—and our hearts went out to these people. We want-ed to help them. There could be no greater inspiration for the World Ride's mission and we took advantage of every opportunity and passing conversation to explain the purpose of our mission and to speak about cancer. It was exactly this sort of place where we were needed the most. Whatever uncomfortable feelings we had about cycling in India were minimal in comparison to the sense of meaningfulness we derived from promoting cancer awareness in this poor country. It made every mile of our Indian route worthwhile.

At one of our rest stops we met a Belgian couple on a motorcycle. They'd been touring for about 18 months, but they'd only been in India a few days and already hated it. The man said, "Life is cheap in India. The Hindus believe in life after life after life, so they don't worry about this one." He said he'd been riding motorcycles for 20 years in such places as Indonesia and Africa, but never had his survival skills been so put to the test as they had been here. He and his wife planned to cut their Indian tour short and leave the country as soon as possible.

At another rest stop, we saw an Indian hairstylist. His shop was a dirt yard where he'd set up a chair and propped a mirror against a tree. I decided I needed a haircut. For 65 cents, it was probably the best haircut I've ever had.

Approaching Moradabad

Just before reaching the city of Moradabad, we stayed at a hotel patrolled by heavily armed guards. Peter, being a military man, took careful note and warned us to be especially careful—no cameras, not too many questions, etc. I'd asked one of the hotel people why the guards were there. He said there were some Indian VIPs staying there that night. I saw that he felt threatened by my questions. Peter's advice sunk in and I heeded it. The guards looked mean, professional, and unlike the police along the roads—

they looked as if they'd happily shoot you on the spot. Peter had understood this at first glance. I hadn't.

Before we left the next morning, a worker at the hotel warned us against terrorists on the road we were scheduled to take. He told us to be sure we stopped riding at sundown.

On the other side of Moradabad we were warned again, this time by a policeman. We were taking a side road to the Nepal border and the policeman told Peter there was rebelliousness in the area we'd be traversing. Two warnings about the same area—we paid attention.

Side road or not, terrorists or no terrorists, it was still a heavily traveled route, still crowded with people who encircled us at every stop. At one point, we decided to ride off into a field for a few moments of relief. Jeff had dropped something, however, and went back for it, telling us to go ahead into the field. We watched him as he came back down the road, and a bunch of people on bikes followed right behind him. The Pied Piper. No way could we avoid these people. On one leg of our journey, a kid kept pace with us for perhaps six miles on a one- or three-speed bike!

Getting Our Message Out

About 80 miles before the Nepalese border, we stopped at a hotel with a sign declaring it to be "Five Star"—however, "One-half-Star" was a more apt designation. There was an Indian in the lobby straight out of a story book. He wore a headdress, white gown, curled-up mustache—pure Kipling. He told us it was election time in the province and that a former Minister of Petroleum was campaigning in the neighborhood for a local candidate. That meant reporters and press, and having done no business for the World Ride in India, I asked the clerk if he could arrange an interview for us with some of the reporters. I showed the clerk our press clippings and explained our mission and he kindly sent someone off to hunt up a reporter. His kindness and eagerness to help was typical of the Indians we met.

My inquiry resulted in being invited to meet with the reporters attending the former Minister's press conference, and it was quite successful. The reporters took down the proper addresses for cancer donations and promised they'd call upon their fellow Indians to raise funds for the cause. It couldn't have gone better. This was a country where communications were so difficult I hadn't been able to pre-arrange Jaycee meetings or avail myself of their press contacts. I was delighted with this last-minute development. The prospect of solid publicity was reinforced that evening when one of the reporters returned with two other reporters for more information. As far as the World Ride's purpose was concerned, this was indeed a "Five-Star" hotel—it catalyzed a good ending to what had been a generally discouraging Indian experience with respect to publicity.

Nepal, the country of Mt. Everest, was just ahead of us. Although we anticipated more terrible roads, we also anticipated a much more expansive landscape as we approached the foothills of the Himalayas—routes going higher and higher, colder, cleaner air and, most of all, fewer people.

Fifteen

ON THE ROAD TO HONG KONG

Nepal/Bangladesh/Hong Kong:
November 11–28

It took us three hours to clear the Nepalese border, the longest and most challenging border delay of the trip. For one thing, the guards were suspicious of my camcorder and held us up to inspect it. Unexpectedly, we next had to get visas, which cost $40 each. I don't think the visas were necessary. Most likely, the money we paid served to fatten the immigration officer's take-home pay that day. During part of the proceedings, the guards called an official who could speak English and we had to wait for him to show up. The final delay was a photographic one—I had no photo for my visa and the immigration officer had to think the matter over. Finally, he accepted a photo from one of our newspaper publicity clippings, and concluded the dealing by asking for a tip. He'd already drained us of $120 in visa fees, so I thought it was more than ample to give him the 55 cents in loose change.

It was already November 11, nine days before our scheduled appearance at the JCI Congress in Hong Kong—we had to get moving.

As we ascended into the higher country of Nepal, the

roads were as bad as they were in India, only a different calibre of bad. Some of the holes were big enough to swallow small cars. Rocks and loose gravel were on the roadbed at every turn, making ordinary cycling a challenge and fast cycling suicidal. The rural areas were sparsely populated, but the towns were as crowded and as noisy as they were in India, and in some areas just as polluted.

More Delays

Because of the long delay at the border and another flat tire, we were at least a day late reaching Dhangadhi in southern Nepal. If we had held to our present progress, we'd have been equally late for our other scheduled stops in Nepal as well as for our arrival in Bangladesh and our flight to Hong Kong. Something had to give.

I suggested to Jeff and Peter that I could go on to Hong Kong alone and that they could continue on the scheduled route through Nepal. They wouldn't hear of it—insisting that we stay together as a team, and I was heartened. In Dhangadhi we decided to shave some time off our journey by taking a bus to Kathmandu, Nepal's capital. This would assure a timely arrival in Hong Kong—if God was willing, that is.

At the hotel we stayed at in Dhangadhi the night before our bus trip, we met a former public school teacher from Boston. He appeared to be in his mid-sixties and was in Nepal as part of the Peace Corps effort. He was a neat guy and we hung out with him that evening. He told us that women volunteers in the Peace Corps had a tough time of it in Nepal because of the prevalent discrimination against women. Many who had journeyed there on a mission of good will had had become frustrated and returned home.

By Bus or Bust

As nearly as I can recall, the bus ride to Kathmandu was about 20 hours, making stops at dozens of little towns. For the most part, the bus route was along narrow, winding, rock-strewn roads through an elevated valley in the Himalayan foothills, the kind of heart-in-your-throat ride that naturally comes to mind when you think of the Third World. It was high country but not mountainous. Although arid from drought and laced by ravines and dry river beds, it was really quite beautiful.

On the bus—an old clunker right out of the Sixties—we were crammed inside with what had to be the absolute maximum number of passengers. A sweeping second hand on a huge, school room-type clock attached to a panel at the front of the bus served to remind us of every second of the interminable ride. The bus's suspension and shocks were totally shot and we felt every inch of the journey. It belched black smoke, wheezed, shivered and teetered. On the outskirts of every one of the towns we stopped at, somebody would get out of the bus and pay what we figured was a tax of some sort before we could proceed.

So it was on roads fit mostly for goats that we headed toward Kathmandu. I had to laugh. It was either that or go bananas.

While in Dhangadhi, I'd called the Vice President of the Junior Chamber International in Kathmandu and he said he'd have someone meet our bus when it arrived. The bus was about two hours late, but there they were, three or four Jaycees waiting for us with fresh flowers. The Chamber had arranged free accommodations for us at a hotel owned by a Jaycee Senator, and after we'd exchanged introductions with our welcoming committee, they took us to the hotel where we immediately slipped into comas from exhaustion.

Hello Kathmandu

Our new itinerary freed us up to spend a few days in Kathmandu, where we were taken to see a real, living goddess who just happened to be a seven-year-old girl. We didn't get the full details on the religious tenets responsible for her being so honored, but she was confined to a temple in the center of Kathmandu and allowed to leave it only on very rare occasions. She was destined to remain in the temple, being considered a living goddess until she "bled for the first time"—as our Jaycee guide delicately stated it. Thereafter she'd probably never marry because men were afraid they'd die if they became involved with someone who had once been a living goddess. Apparently, she was very rarely seen by ordinary citizens, but we were fortunate to have the JCI Vice President with us who repeatedly called up to her until she appeared at the temple window.

We also attended a sister-city renewal ceremony between the Kathmandu Junior Chamber and a visiting delegation of Jaycee members from a Japanese city. The Kathmandu mayor spoke at the ceremony and after duly praising the brotherly connection between the sister-city Chambers, he proceeded to espouse the political platform that got him elected—"Clean, green, healthy Kathmandu."

Now, there was a challenge! Kathmandu was, hands-down, the most polluted city we had visited. The air was so foul it had made me ill and I had to wear a filter-mask to avoid further getting sicker. The mayor's environmental rally cry at the Jaycee ceremony demonstrated how he counted on the Jaycees as an ally in his efforts.

The Nepalese Jaycees had already accomplished several community miracles and I'd bet on them to accomplish more. In the nearby community of Bhaktapur, the Jaycees had started a school and a small cancer hospital. Most likely because of the pollution, the incidence of cancer was high in the area. We were impressed. The Nepal Jaycees were doing many positive things and they were also very active in the Junior Chamber International. The President of the Nepal Junior Chamber, in fact, was running for the office of Vice President of the JCI and was preparing for his trip to the JCI Congress in Hong Kong.

On to Bangladesh

We flew from Kathmandu to Dacca, the capital of Bangladesh. Dacca was like New Delhi, which in turn was like Kathmandu—which pretty much says it all. About the only thing worthy of reporting was that I had my first rickshaw ride, and how a sleazy guy tried to sell me some hashish before he was chased off by a hotel guard. Jeff and Peter had opted to stay at a respectable hotel, but my budget wouldn't bear it, so I ended up in a poorer section of town. Frankly, I enjoyed the privacy and was able to work on my speech for the Hong Kong Conference. The challenge facing me was to compress five months worth of our World Ride road experiences into a three-and-a-half-minute talk.

I met up with Peter and Jeff the next morning and we went to the airport in the early evening and spent the night in the waiting area. The doors to the airport building were locked, and entrance was allowed only by armed guards. Well into the night we saw large numbers of destitute people milling around outside, staring through the windows with vacant expressions. No planes were landing or taking off, nobody had to be delivered or picked up—there was no reason for such a crowd. We could only conclude that these people lived here. Whatever the case, they clearly had no homes for the night—yet another link in the long chain of human sorrow that pervaded the subcontinent of Asia.

Hong Kong—At Last!

Arriving at Hong Kong, we bicycled 10 miles or so to the downtown area of the city where the Junior Chamber International had booked us a large room for a week at the

YMCA. Whatever image you may have of a YMCA, forget it. This YMCA was equivalent to a four-star hotel—a traveler's Mecca. It was 15 to 20 stories high and as modern as the 21st Century—with every imaginable convenience and luxury.

Immediately after settling in and making ourselves respectable for a change, I began the business of renewing Jaycee acquaintances, making new ones and bringing everyone up to date on the World Ride's experiences. Several of the Jaycees who'd been so kind to us in their countries during our ride were there and were glad to see we'd arrived safely. They'd been worried about us and we were touched by their obvious concern. The gathering had the feeling of a warm family reunion, and certainly qualified as the major highlight of our travels to date. I loved every moment, and was especially thankful to have the opportunity to express the team's gratitude to the many, many Jaycees who had supported us and looked after us. It was certainly their World Ride as much as ours.

Among those present at the Congress were Desmond Alufahi and Tom Clear. Desmond was the Massachusetts Jaycee who essentially got the World Ride's wheels moving by pointing us to Tom, who in turn extended the official invitation to Travis Ebel and myself to make the World Ride presentation to the Junior Chamber International in Coral Gables, FL. I also had a chance to express my appreciation to Robby Dawkins, President of the JCI, and to dozens of Junior Chamber executives and Board members.

Our Dream Already Half-Realized

At this point, the World Ride had a track record—we'd ridden about 6,600 miles, just about half of the 13,665 miles we were to eventually cover. It was a great feeling to be able to share our accomplishments with the Jaycees rather than just our hopes—especially with Alex MacDonald, the former Vice President of the JCI, who was directly involved in the successful strategy of the World Ride from start to finish.

Nancy arrived as promised—the third time she'd flown to join me on the World Ride. She was to stay a long, wonderful week filled with sight-seeing, Jaycee parties and quiet times together. Whatever I've said about my feelings for her in the earlier chapters goes double in this one—she literally had come half-way around the world to support me and the project. I wanted her to have a great week—and she did.

She'd also brought the 15-minute video presentation tape with her. I made the presentation, along with my brief speech on behalf of the team, on November 25, 1993. Appropriately, it was Thanksgiving Day in the U.S. When I was finished, Robby Dawkins, the JCI President, presented each member of the team with a pair of commemorative cuff links and thanked us on behalf of the Congress. I couldn't help thinking, as I looked across the large hall filled with Jaycees—so many of whom had supported us—that the thanks should have gone the other way. I had done my best to say so in my speech, but if I'd spoken for an hour I don't think I could have adequately expressed the team's gratitude.

After the meeting, I had a chance to talk with the President of the U.S. Junior Chamber of Commerce, Matt Shapiro, and with the Executive Vice President, Steve Lawson. I also made contacts with Jaycees whose cities and areas would be on upcoming routes. From my conversations with them, and having heard my speech and seen the video, they'd been given a good idea of what the World Ride entailed and how much we appreciated and depended on them for support. We still had eight countries to go, including a west-to-east ride across the U.S. The contacts we made here would certainly help assure the success of the next 7,000 miles.

Onward to Korea

Nancy left on Sunday, November 28, just about an hour before the World Ride team boarded a plane to leave for Seoul, South Korea. It was hard to leave her, but from Hong Kong forward I'd be riding toward her, not away—a thought that did much to keep my spirits up.

Jeff and Peter brought up the point that we'd be in South Korea and Japan as winter approached—which was no time to be on a bike—and suggested we shave a few days off our stay in there. I felt reluctant about the suggestion, feeling that these were promising places for us to raise money for cancer research. Our planned itinerary had called for eight days in South Korea and 14 days in Japan.

We voted and the odd-man-out process went against me and I suggested a compromise—spending six or seven days in South Korea and seven or eight in Japan. They agreed and it turned out to be adequate time to do what was needed.

As it turned out, the weather was as cold as Jeff and Peter had predicted, contributing to a flu-like virus that attacked and weakened all of us—making it doubtful that we could have stuck to our original itinerary even if we had planned to.

Sixteen

EASTERN WAYS

South Korea/Japan:
November 28–December 13

In South Korea and Japan, we were generally addressed as "Mister." This was followed by our first name only—Mr. Jeff, Mr. Peter and Mr. Richard. I therefore introduce you to Mr. Sung.

The South Korean Junior Chamber decided to finance every expense for the World Ride in South Korea. They also decided to send one of their staff members along—with a pocketful of money—to accompany us every inch of the way in a support vehicle. The man they chose was Mr. Sung. We first met him at a Jaycee breakfast on the morning after our arrival and a blissful night's sleep in what had to be one of Seoul's very best hotels. A happy, beaming young man in his mid-twenties, Mr. Sung was decked out in a business suit and tie (the South Koreans were at all times very efficient and business-minded), and his escort vehicle was decorated with a World Ride banner. Very elegant.

Mr. Sung: Guide and Friend

So, out we went into South Korea, escorted through Seoul traffic by Mr. Sung in what had now become a cold, almost freezing rain. My fingers became so numb I had to ask him for a pair of gloves. At least Jeff and I were in long pants, but Peter, not having brought a pair, had to settle for shorts.

The South Korean Jaycees had organized our World Ride in their country with awesome precision. There were two guys in the escort car: Mr. Sung and an associate. About every 60 miles or so the escort car would be met by another escort car. Mr. Sung would switch to the new car, and off we'd go on the next leg, Mr. Sung faithfully accompanying us and directing us in accord with his plans and schedules. At appropriate times, he would yell to us out his car (in the most friendly way), "Now we eat!" Then he'd steer us to a place for lunch where there'd often be Jaycees to greet us. We'd talk with them a bit, meet with reporters if they were there and Mr. Sung would pay for the lunch. Then he'd say, "Now we must ride more!"

This sort of thing would go on all day until he'd finally announce, "Okay, now we sleep."

Keeping Us Going

Like a good executive, Mr. Sung kept us on schedule by having everything fully programmed and prepared—it was a pleasure. All we had to do was follow this guy and not worry about a thing. He was good humored and always laughing and he took sensationally good care of us. We enjoyed the pampering and there wasn't a complaint to be heard—not a chance.

One of the support-vehicle drivers, who stayed with us the longest and who kindly hosted Mr. Sung and the team at his own home one night, was Mr. Ko. His car was equipped with a police siren. Mr. Ko would pull ahead of us at big intersections, he and Mr. Sung laughing away like crazy, and they'd wind up the siren and cars would screech to a halt while we pedaled our way through—now how can you not love guys like Mr. Sung and Mr. Ko?

Press coverage, as you might expect, was equally efficient and omnipresent. Many of the reporters and Jaycees, incidentally, spoke impeccable English, another great plus for communication and efficiency. This was especially gratifying, because we were working our tails off in the cold and rain.

Food, in South Korea, was primarily fish and rice. When we stayed at Mr. Ko's house, however, his wife had surprised us with a breakfast of meat stew. Whether this was a Korean custom, or just a generous nod to what she thought might be our Western tastes, I don't know. It was heavy—but it was delicious and I don't remember leaving any of it on my plate.

Gracious Guests

Throughout our World Ride we made it a point to eat whatever was served to us. Food was our fuel and it didn't pay to be too fussy when the only thing available to us in some of the cultures we encountered was unfamiliar with our usual eating customs. Not only would a refusal to eat be inexcusably uncomplimentary to our host or hostess, it also could be costly to us in terms of energy and health. There was a survival aspect to it that became an instinct, and I suspect that many fussy eaters would find themselves quickly cured of that trait were they to travel and live as we did on the World Ride.

I might mention that we were in South Korea during the height of the U.S.-North Korean negotiations over the latter's disposition of nuclear materials. At that time, it was seen as an extremely volatile and dangerous situation, especially for the South Koreans whose country could be decimated if war erupted. There were many predictions in South Korean news reports of a likely, perhaps imminent, conflict. We didn't talk much about it with our South Korean hosts, but it was most definitely on the team's mind and we were admittedly uneasy about it.

Our departure from South Korea, however, was brought about by another kind of war—our bodies fighting a flu-like virus that became steadily worse as we traveled southward and which eventually laid all three of us out for a day in Taegu. We were scheduled to go on to Pusan and we were seriously considering it, virus or no virus, when we saw heavy snow flurries. That decided it. It was time to pack it in and we knew it.

Goodbye, Friend

Mr. Sung had witnessed our biking struggles first-hand—the lousy weather and our increasing illness. He'd drawn very close to the team as a friend, and he said something to us that was amazing. "Geez," he said, "I wish I could stick with you." I don't think I've ever been quite as touched as I was by those few words from this happy-go-lucky guy who lived half a world away from me and whom I'd only met a few days earlier. I've never heard a clearer expression of closeness and brotherhood. A most unusual guy, this Mr. Sung.

We had dinner with the Jaycees that night in Taegu (the same South Korean city which, at this writing, had just suffered through an enormous gas explosion that killed many South Koreans, becoming a major international news story). The three of us were feeling really terrible from the virus, and the next day we took a plane back to Seoul, the Jaycees again generously picking up the cost.

Business Cards and Bowing

Before we left Taegu, we were given several business cards by the Jaycees—a common occurrence throughout our South Korean visit. But these cards and the customs that accompanied them were special. The cards were gorgeously designed, featuring a full-color photo of the cardowner, and resumes of the bearer's social and business status. It was a serious matter, this giving out business cards, and it would be an affront to just accept it with a quick glance and put it in your pocket as we do in the U.S. The recipient was expected to receive the card graciously and spend some time examining it, commenting appropriately and showing respect for the bearer, his title and the company he worked for. This was one of the social dynamics we had to learn.

Another dynamic was the art of bowing: Your host bows,

you bow, or vice versa. But then its over. My father, who often dealt with Asians in his business, told me that when he was new to the bowing protocol, he didn't know when to stop his bowing and the exchange went on interminably. He was amused when he told me about it, but I could sense that he didn't find it at all funny at the time.

I think the team handled the protocols of the South Korean trip pretty well, and I suspect we left Taegu for Seoul with good impressions lingering behind us—and the same when we left Seoul for Tokyo. I know the South Koreans made an outstanding impression on us. Despite cultural and other differences, the South Korean Jaycees embraced the World Ride mission, made it known in their country, covered its costs, provided escorts and gave us unsurpassed organizational and moral support. Mr. Sung, alone, had already earned them our everlasting esteem.

Our Time in Tokyo

Takashi Nakao (Mr. Takashi, that is) was our contact in Tokyo, and after a fast-food stop (heavy noodle soup being traditional rather than hamburgers and fries), he escorted us to the home of Mr. and Mrs. Hayafuni. We were greeted by their son, Mr. Masafumi, a Jaycee and the president of the family company—a prosperous flower farm. After removing our sneakers, we walked into a magnificent home of polished woods and delicate furniture—we felt we entered a small, exquisite museum.

I extended my hand to our hostess, Mr. Masafumi's

mother (a woman of about 60), and instantly realized my mistake—one may shake the hand of a man, but never the hand of an older woman. She was startled and drew back, but I quickly bowed and I'm sure she forgave me for my heathen western ways. (I, in turn, forgave the Hayafunis for a shower-stall nozzle that was at the level of my chest.)

Japan, like South Korea, was a modern, wealthy, disciplined society. Despite the overcrowding that is common in southeast Asia, Japan was a well-ordered, non-intrusive, clean and well-kept nation. ("Immaculate" was a word that occurred to me many times in my Japanese travels.) It's affluence—or at least relative affluence—was striking.

This was true not only among the Jaycees we met, but in the general sense of things as we took note of the people and our surroundings. One young man we spoke with, for example, had a luxury four-wheel-drive truck with an expensive satellite tracking device in his cab that plotted his exact location on a map. In some of the countries we'd ridden through, such material possessions by a commoner, let alone his access to such technology, was unimaginable.

Another illustration of the well-monied Japanese society is the cost of Jaycee membership—in Japan, it is about $2,000 a year. (In contrast, it costs approximately $40 to $50 to become a Jaycee back in Massachusetts.)

After my stooped-over shower at the Hayafunis, several Jaycees arrived and took us out to dinner in Tokyo and then on to a karaoke bar in a part of Tokyo noted for its sex shops. This wasn't like 42nd Street in New York, however. It was clean, orderly and well-mannered with the ... uh ...

merchants politely pointing to photographs of their women and inviting us to partake. I guess you could call it a non-seedy red-light district. And I guess you could also assume that this is where many Western male guests liked to be taken when visiting Tokyo. (For any friends and family of Jeff, Peter and Richard who may be reading, let it be known that if our low interest level had been typical, the merchants would have had to find another line of work.)

Everybody took turns singing in the karaoke bar—the results of our efforts being rated by an electronic system—and it was amazing how really good some of the patrons sounded. Takashi was running around taking pictures of everything, and while it is true that my electronic rating was about dead zero, it was a great evening in good company and easily the highlight of my time in Japan.

Taking Off

We were given a starting-line ceremony the next morning, complete with press coverage and photographers. A manufacturer's promotional representative, Mr. Takao, gave us gifts of long bicycle tights and some really good jackets and other items to keep us dry and comfy. An "early Christmas", as Jeff said, and we were very grateful for them in the near-freezing weather. (So was Mr. Takao, what with having his products shown in the newspaper photos.)

Mr. Takashi bicycled with us through Tokyo proper, and his son was given the keys to Mr. Takashi's car—I think it was one of the youngster's first solos behind the wheel. All of our belongings were in the car and he promptly got himself lost, failing to meet us at the designated spot on the outskirts of town. He appeared after three hours, but you can imagine how concerned we all were. I could not have imagined anything worse than having a serious accident befall someone as a direct result of supporting the World Ride team. It was one of my worst scares of the whole trip.

As in South Korea, our route in Japan was to the south, and we were again struck by the orderly and tidy nature of the Japanese. Fields, paddies, woods—all of it as well-groomed and tended as a park. While traffic could be heavy at times, we never had a sense of chaos or undue danger. There was never a hint of rowdyism or roadside beggars or any of the other unpleasant things we had come to expect from our Asian travels. South Korea and Japan were much alike in providing civilized comforts. Hotels were clean and neat, well-managed and welcoming and with every modern convenience. Food stores were everywhere, well-stocked with an amazing variety of good things, and bike shops and telephones and other necessities bike travelers take for granted in the U.S., we could take for granted here, too. I'd recommend a bicycle tour of Japan to anyone—but be prepared for high prices.

Mount Fuji Country

On December 7—Pearl Harbor Day in the U.S.—we were in the city of Yazu. It was cloudy and bitterly cold and the terrain was mountainous. This was Mount Fuji country and we had almost given up hope of even glimpsing this most majestic of Japanese landmarks when the clouds suddenly lifted and we were treated to a magnificent view of the entire mountain. Road signs in this mountainous, winding-road region were printed in Japanese only and not very helpful to us. We were continually comparing the signs with our map to line up whatever similarities we might spot that would enable us to stay on course. It was quite a jigsaw puzzle, and success often relied upon the matching-up of one or two odd-looking Japanese characters.

Mr. Takashi had thoughtfully planned our Japanese route to provide us with memorable views of his homeland, but some of the legs he'd programmed were far too long for the time he'd allotted. We had to short-circuit some of them to be on time for meetings he set up with Jaycees. One such realignment occurred at Irako, near the mouth of a large bay that extended some 50 miles inland. Mr. Takashi had expected us to bike around the edge of the bay to a point on the opposite shore—maybe 150-200 miles—but it was impossible to do and still keep our scheduled appointments. Instead, we opted to ferry across from Irako and we worked with Mr. Takashi to communicate our route changes so the Jaycees we were to meet wouldn't be inconvenienced.

Irako was a small village catering largely to tourists—a lovely little enclave of shops and homes overlooking the sparkling Pacific on one side and the princely bay on the other. As we slowly biked through the village, several women standing outside of a shop waved us over and offered us free food. I had no idea what this was all about, but free food is free food, and we went in and dined. While we were munching away, I nearly choked when one of the women came up with some World Ride posters! It turned out that they were connected with the local Jaycees in nearby Tahara. The President of the Tahara Jaycees, Mr. Sumu, had given them the posters and alerted them to our coming and they had prepared for us, even readying overnight accommodations for the team in a small tourist hotel they operated above the shop!

Mr. Sumu arrived later that evening, spending some time with us, and in the morning he kindly presented us with free ferry tickets. A woman associate of his, Ms. Yuko, had written a note to us, in English, a copy of which she gave to each member of the World Ride team, and it read as follows:

> *I'm glad to meet you. I was deeply moved by your activities.*
> *I wish your success. Hold out. Have a nice trip.*

She dated the note and signed it, adding, "Funny Japanese girl." On the other side of the note was a brief lesson in Japanese, teaching us how to say "thank you", "good afternoon" and "good evening"—"arigato", "konnichiwa" and "konbanwa," respectively.

I'm not easily charmed, but Ms. Yuko's note managed to do the trick.

Remembering Kobe

Our bikes had become progressively worse in Japan. The rain and the cold and our weakened condition from the virus we'd contracted in South Korea didn't make things any easier. On our way to Osaka, our last destination in Japan, our miseries were so obvious that a passing motorist rolled his window down and compassionately handed us a can of hot coffee.

In Osaka, we were hosted by Mr. Yasumi of the Osaka Junior Chamber. During our stay, he arranged for us to meet with fellow Chamber members in nearby Kobe and I have vivid recollections of that bustling city and its many impressive construction projects. Sadly, the Kobe earthquake, in which more than 5,000 died and destruction ran into the billions, was the major news story of January, 1995, only 13 months after my visit. I was stunned by the television news footage of areas I had visited or which had been pointed out to me with great pride by my Japanese hosts. I had no way of knowing that when I left Kobe and returned to Osaka—to board our plane for Brisbane, Australia—that I'd never be able to return to the same sights I had just left; nor, perhaps would I be able to return to all of the same people.

I think of our World Ride contacts and supporters as part of a far-flung family. The decimation visited upon these kind and gentle people has been an almost impossible thing to reconcile.

Seventeen

THE OTHER SIDE OF WINTER

Australia/New Zealand:
December 14–February 4

We were to spend more than four weeks in Australia and three weeks in New Zealand.

December through February are summer months in the southern latitudes. The weather we encountered was mostly warm and dry and, in terms of riding, probably the most enjoyable months of the trip. In some spots, however, Australia was actually too hot, causing many problems with our tires—even our tube patches wouldn't hold in the excessive heat—and I was continually protecting myself with Shaklee sunscreen lotion. But the fiercely hot days were rare, and were still preferable to painful riding in the near-freezing rains of Japan.

In Australia, we generally followed coastal routes from Bundaberg (200 miles north of Brisbane) to Melbourne, about 1200 miles to the south. Our pace was leisurely, usually 60 or 70 miles a day, and every fifth day, on average, was a rest day. Major repair work on our bikes was done in Bundaberg (all three of us, I think, had been down to one operating gear in Japan), and you can imagine what a pleasure it was to start out in Australia in summer sunshine, on seemingly new bikes, and with a stress-free schedule ahead of us.

No Worries, Mate

When we had landed at Brisbane, we were met by Peter Wilkes of the North Brisbane Junior Chamber. He drove us to his home, where he helped us wash off our bikes, and where we were joined by Des Kinne, our Australian Project Manager. Des had graciously driven down from Bundaberg to meet us and then driven us back to that city for the start of our Australian itinerary.

He arranged great accommodations for me with Tom and Glenda, Bundaberg Jaycees, and for Jeff and Peter with other Jaycees. Tom and Glenda's home was in the rural outskirts of Bundaberg, complete with wild kangaroos skipping across their yard. Unfortunately, these were to be the only live kangaroos I remember seeing in Australia. The many others I saw were along the roadside, quite dead, I'm afraid, from being struck by cars and trucks.

Des and the Bundaberg Jaycees had scheduled some good media coverage for our visit, and this attentiveness to publicity and to the fund-raising mission of the World Ride was to be evident at almost every stop along our Australian and New Zealand routes. Local Jaycees really had their minds on the World Ride project and it made every mile of biking in these countries extremely worthwhile.

World Ride Against Cancer Day

In Gympie, Australia, for example, our Jaycee host was a woman named Lynne, and when we got to talking that evening she suggested a World Ride Against Cancer Day. She wanted it to be an annual event sponsored by the Junior Chamber International in as many countries as possible. Activities would include local bike-riding and racing with proceeds going to cancer research (an idea also suggested previously by Jeff MacInnis, a World Ride adviser). "World Ride Against Cancer Day" is a promising idea with serious fund-raising potential, and I hope to explore it with the Jaycees, or perhaps other interested sponsors, in the coming months.

Our Australian route took us back through Brisbane and then on to Murwillumbah (town names in Australia were a constant source of fascination, and even more so in New Zealand). I'd been sure that plans had been made for the Jaycees to meet us in Murwillumbah, but when we got into the town there was no Jaycee in sight and so I made a call to our local contact. He was surprised we were there, but using what by now had become a familiar Australian expression to us, he said, "No worries, mate!" He showed up about a half-hour later, escorted us to a nearby Jaycee's home, knocked on the door, explained who we were and what the World Ride was all about and that we needed a place to bunk for the night. We were invited in, fed and given rooms for the night—three total strangers! We were impressed!

Australians remind me very much of Americans. I've heard that thought expressed by others, and now I know why. Aussies are easy to meet—friendly, open, interested in everything, very sports-minded, up-to-date on modern technology. They were like us in their mannerisms, in their reactions, in the way they approached things. If it weren't for their "Down Under" accents, I wouldn't have been able to tell them apart from my neighbors in Massachusetts. I didn't have this feeling in the other countries we'd visited—there was always something distinct about other people, even the Scots and British—but there was the immediate feeling of being among family with Australians.

How I Spent Christmas

On December 24, Christmas Eve, the World Ride team arrived in Yamba. There were no Jaycees here, and although we could have made other arrangements for the holidays—many Jaycees would have gladly welcomed us into their homes—we decided not to.

Peter and Jeff, feeling the need to treat themselves to a little Christmas luxury, opted to stay in an upscale campground that was a little too rich for my meager budget, so I decided to find my own accommodations. But that wasn't my only reason for leaving them—I really felt the need for some private spiritual communion.

I had decided to seek out a church. I wanted to get off by myself, thank God for watching over us on our World

Ride, and I wanted to find a place to do it quietly and properly. I was extraordinarily thankful, and very conscious of the spiritual vacuum in the hectic demands of our itinerary.

There weren't too many houses of worship in this coastal village, and being a Protestant I went up to an Episcopal church, but the door was locked. The next church I saw was Catholic, and this was clearly open—a couple was coming out of the sanctuary. I introduced myself, told them about the World Ride and that I just wanted to sleep out in a church on that Christmas Eve. In an instant, they introduced me to Father Daisy. He listened to my story, laughed, and pointed to a steep hill near the church. "Meet me on top of that hill," he said.

Doing as I was told, I soon arrived at the "Star of the Sea Convent" and there was Father Daisy huddling with the Sisters and making arrangements for me to stay the night. They showed me to a room that offered exactly the spiritual sanctuary I needed—simple, clean, unadorned. Here I could concentrate on long-posponed prayers of gratitude and appreciation. I was shown the way to a shower and then invited to dinner, where I did my best to eat like a normal human being rather than a famished bicycle rider.

In the morning, I attended their public Christmas Mass and was then invited to share Christmas dinner with several nuns and priests. This was a truly festive occasion. Wine was in abundance and everyone joined in on such songs as "Waltzing Matilda"—a song you've never really heard until you've heard it sung by several nuns and priests in a convent on top of a windy hill on Christmas Day in Yamba, Australia.

This may have been the most meaningful and wonderful Christmas I have ever experienced. If the spirit of that day is measured by helping hands, the welcoming of a stranger and love toward one another, it was indeed just that.

Cycling Down the East Coast

The team spent New Year's Eve in Sydney—magnificent fireworks exploded over the harbor in a clear night sky, couples were holding hands, some were dancing. It could have been Boston or Seattle. It was almost impossible to believe I was literally half a world away from home. As I've said, there is little sense of apartness when an American is among the Australians. You'll see for yourself when you go there.

Leaving Sydney, we headed south to Melbourne, stopping at several towns along the way, including Ballarat. It was here that I caught up on a lot of paperwork, made another of my several calls to KISS 108 FM in Boston (with an update on the World Ride's progress) and telephoned Nancy. She said she'd do her best to meet up with me in New Zealand, something we'd planned, but depended on some financial details being worked out. With high hopes for that meeting, and with everything else going smoothly, we left Ballarat for Melbourne, and it was on this leg that we had the worst accident of our trip.

The Accident

We were riding at a particularly fast clip down a long incline when it appeared certain that a car coming off a feeder road ahead of us would merge onto the highway just as we passed the road. We'd been riding one behind the other—Peter in front, then Jeff, then me—and we'd all been keeping an eye on that car and gauging our chances of getting across the intersection before the car did.

Peter was the first to decide we couldn't make it and he braked fairly severely. Jeff, following him closely, and with his eyes on the car rather than on Peter, rode full-tilt into the rear of Peter's bike and was thrown onto the pavement, landing hard on his head and shoulder. His Vetta helmet (we all wore Vetta helmets) saved him from what could have been terrible, even fatal, injury, but he was badly shaken and quite scraped up. He had a serious bump on his shoulder and he was hurting severely in several places.

Peter—ever-prepared for such incidents—applied alcohol swabs and bandaged Jeff up. After a brief rest, Jeff was able to ride the 20 miles or so to our next scheduled stop just outside of Melbourne, but he had to go slowly and he could barely use his left hand. He was not a happy camper, but he had tremendous courage and team spirit.

Lynne—the woman who had suggested the World Ride Against Cancer Day—had a sister, Jenny, who had agreed to accommodate us when we arrived. Jenny was a nurse, and when she met us near Melbourne she took Jeff to a hospital for a proper medical inspection. It turned out that

Jeff had torn a ligament in his left shoulder and that he'd have to stay off his bike for a week or two, or perhaps much longer, depending on how the healing progressed.

He was delivered back to us with his left arm in a sling, and while he bemoaned the fact that he couldn't ride, he didn't seem to mind Jenny's pampering one bit. She was a very good-looking woman, and I've sometimes wondered if Jeff wouldn't have preferred to have been left in Melbourne for his recuperation. I'm sure he could have stretched it out over a few months.

Anyway, we were all very thankful that Jeff's injuries weren't more serious. Having seen every moment of his spill, at the time I wasn't at all sure he was ever going to be riding another mile with us.

On to New Zealand

New Zealand is composed of two large islands, the North Island and the South Island. We departed Melbourne and arrived in Auckland, on the North Island, on January 16. We had a prestigious welcoming committee: Chris, the President of the Junior Chamber of New Zealand; Karen, a Regional Governor of the North Island; and Murray, our World Ride Project Manager in New Zealand. The three of us were fitted into various cars and whisked away to Karen's house where Murray and I and other Jaycees discussed our New Zealand itinerary and acquiring a rental support vehicle for Jeff.

It was the height of the tourist season, mind you, but

on my second call to a car rental agency I talked to a man named Kevin. He listened to my explanation of the World Ride mission, heard my tale of woe about Jeff, and said on behalf of Henderson's Car Rental he'd be glad to donate a support vehicle for such a worthy cause! The New Zealand Jaycees agreed to pay for the cost of insurance—so we had a free support vehicle for our three-week stay in New Zealand! I promised Kevin we'd get Henderson's Car Rental a good bit of publicity for his generosity, and I fulfilled that pledge in interviews during our stay in New Zealand.

I called Nancy, assuring her of a car, and she said the personal financial stuff had been solved and that she'd be coming to New Zealand in about a week. (She had an aunt and uncle in New Zealand who she had not seen in many years and whose home was almost directly on our scheduled route, and we joined them for a few great meals and spent the night with her cousins.)

Karen arranged for the team to attend a barbecue in a nearby town at the home of a JCI Senator. The special guest of the evening was the Finance Minister of New Zealand—a matter of some excitement among the local Jaycees. I was told that one of the reasons he came to the barbecue was because he was interested in the World Ride's mission and wanted to lend his support to raise awareness and funds for cancer research.

It was a big party, with media coverage, and it was helpful to the World Ride in another way, too. Gary, one of the public relations people for the New Zealand Jaycees, had come to the barbecue and agreed to prepare a question-and-answer outline with me, which he would then forward it to the media along our intended route. In this way, the media would have advance information about the World Ride, with most of their questions answered for them. This was extremely useful to us, saving many hours of interview time, and it assured us of more accurate advance publicity.

Our New Zealand route was largely along the coast, the roads never far from the sight of water in this island nation. Peter had once walked its length and longed to settle here. To me, it had the feeling of a new land in many ways—clean, pristine, fresh. At once steep and dramatic, and then rolling and soft, dotted with countless sheep pastures, close-cropped hillsides and valleys, rushing streams, quiet lakes—it was sheer joy to travel through a country like this. And so very worthwhile for our work in cancer awareness and funding. As in Australia, the World Ride was well received, welcomed and publicized throughout New Zealand. Funds were raised and T-shirts sold, even at impromptu stops and casual get-togethers. The Jaycees were marvelous, and their country was beautiful. If Peter does go back and settle in New Zealand, I'd understand why and be glad for him.

Nancy in New Zealand

Nancy arrived on January 25, and what I remember the most fondly are the many long walks we took. New Zealand is a country made for walking and picnicking and for sitting somewhere high up, with long views of the sea. The World Ride had its schedule to keep, of course, and Nancy and Jeff would accompany us in the support vehicle.

In a few days, it seemed as if Nancy had never left us in Hong Kong and had been right here all the time, as much a part of the team as Jeff, Peter or myself. She joined in on our decisions and plans, and spent many hours bringing us up to date on World Ride affairs in the States. To this day, I'm still surprised when I connect her with such oddly-named places as Waipukurau, Rotorua, Matta Matta and a dozen other unlikely New Zealand town names when the only place I went to sleep thinking about during most of the trip was Milton, Massachusetts.

February 4 was the team's day to leave Auckland for Argentina but, because of plane schedules, Nancy was to stay in New Zealand another day. Although I'd be leaving, Nancy was happy to have been invited by our gracious hosts, Roseann Gedye, a JCI Vice President, and her husband, Steve, for a day of boating in Auckland harbor.

Roseann and I met in Coral Gables, Fla., during the Massachusetts Jaycee presentation to the JCI Executive Committee. In fact, she was the reason I put New Zealand on the World Ride route. She is the very embodiment of all that is great about New Zealanders, and, like me, she had lost close family to cancer and had a great deal of empathy with the World Ride mission. So, I would be leaving Nancy in wonderful hands.

Nancy and I walked several miles on our last day together, browsed through some stores, listened to music and generally cheered each other up as best we could. These partings were hard to take, but we were on the downhill leg of the World Ride, more than 9,000 miles were behind us, less than 5,000 to go, and in a few days we'd at least be in the same hemisphere. In fact, the last leg of the World Ride trip was to be across the United States—from Los Angeles to Boston. Only another month away from being practically in Nancy's backyard.

So we focused on that, and we talked about meeting in New Mexico for Nancy's birthday. We hugged before I boarded the plane to Argentina—then I was on my way to yet another continent.

Eighteen

26 DAYS IN SOUTH AMERICA

Argentina/Uruguay/Brazil:
February 4–March 1

We left Auckland at 11 p.m. on February 4. Flying east, we'd reached Buenos Aires at 5:30 p.m. on the same day. Jet lag was ferocious; the only thing on earth I wanted to do was sleep. But we were met at the airport by Nicholas Gonzalez, President of the Junior Chamber of Argentina, and were instantly whisked off for an interview at Argentina's No.1 television station for some country-wide publicity. Exhausted or not, this was a major opportunity for the World Ride mission, and I have to admit that it woke me up in a hurry. Nicholas had been right on the ball, and this was no time for me to drop it.

Nicholas was also the Director of Civil Defense in Argentina, and following the TV interview he introduced us to Mary Luce, a woman who worked for him, and who generously donated her apartment to the team. After showering at the apartment, we were treated to a marvelous dinner by Nicholas and his wife, Nora. (Dinner was at 9 p.m., almost as late as in Spain.) By midnight our brains were barely functioning and we at last passed out in our beds. If there'd been a country-wide earthquake on that night I doubt we would have noticed it.

Promises to Keep

We stayed in Buenos Aires until February 9, and my time was largely occupied with catch-up administrative work. I had to make a decision about possibly skipping the scheduled South American itinerary and returning to Massachusetts to help coordinate the 3500-mile ride across the U.S. from Los Angeles to Boston. This final part of the World Ride provided the best chance of raising substantial funds for cancer research and there were still many matters of promotion, itinerary and organization that had to be worked out.

Time was growing short, and I felt an urgency to be in the U.S. It was a serious dilemma, and on February 8, I went so far as to exchange my United Airlines ticket for a March flight from Rio de Janeiro to Los Angeles, to a next-day flight from Buenos Aires to Boston.

However, after long telephone talks with Nancy over the next two days, I decided to stay with our South American schedule. She helped me realize that an early return might be interpreted as a failure to fulfill the World Ride pledge. To jump ship now would mean that the Ride would not have been carried out as promised and would inevitably disappoint supporters.

Doing The Right Thing

No matter how legitimate the reasons for coming to Boston might be, how firmly focused I might be on what was best for the World Ride mission of promoting cancer awareness and acquiring research funds, our early return to Boston would be viewed as the failure of Richard Drorbaugh to do what he said he was going to do.

That did it. Case closed. I totally agreed. Everything Nancy said had crossed my mind countless times in the past few days as I had wrestled with this dilemma. But Nancy put it all in perspective: Both responsibilities had to be met; first finishing the ride as planned and then I could become involved with promoting awareness and fund-raising when I got to Los Angeles. (My revised schedule called for 10 days or so in the Los Angeles area before starting out on the cross-U.S. ride; it would have to be enough to get things organized and coordinated.) I simply could not return early and chance the possibility of anyone saying the World Ride had failed to accomplish its bicycling goal! I stayed in South America.

With only minutes to spare, I managed to have my airline ticket changed back to its original status. Then I biked about 100 yards to the ferry terminal where I met up with Jeff and Peter. From there, we were transported across the Rio de la Plata to Montevideo, Uruguay for the real start of our South American biking.

To the White House via Montevideo

Juan and several other Jaycees met us in Montevideo, hosting us for the night, and the next day we met with Larry, the Cultural Affairs Director for the U.S. Embassy in

Uruguay. I was hoping that a U.S. Embassy contact might be able to arrange a meeting with President Clinton or Vice-President Gore on our U.S. leg of the World Ride. Despite my decision to continue the South American schedule, I was still doing some heavy thinking about U.S. publicity for our cancer crusade.

Larry agreed to write a letter of support for the World Ride and to let the President and Vice President know that we were requesting a meeting. He asked us to come back the next day for a copy of the letter he'd be sending and to meet the U.S. Ambassador to Uruguay.

The following day, Sylvia, the National Junior Chamber President of Uruguay, Larry, Jeff, Peter and I met with the Ambassador who was very cordial and encouraging. The Ambassador approved Larry's forwarding of the letter, and he suggested we call him when we were within two weeks of arriving in Arkansas (President Clinton's home state), and to call him again when we were nearing Washington, D.C. He said if we'd alert him as suggested, he'd see what he could do at those times to set up a meeting. He believed that President Clinton probably wouldn't mind breaking up his day for five minutes or so to give his support to the World Ride's mission to fight cancer.

With high hopes and a great sense of accomplishment, we felt no guilt about attending a grand barbecue in our honor, taking in the sights of Carnival days and generally enjoying the effervescent hospitality of the Jaycees for another day or two. Montevideo was a good stop, and after saying our "thank yous" we headed out on our bikes for northern Uruguay and Brazil. Jeff mounted up for the first time since his Australian accident and looked as fit as we were. In a few miles, we were to encounter another accident—not a physical one this time—but the most heartbreaking of the trip. At least for me.

No Camera, No Diary

After pausing to snap a picture of a man with some horses north of Montevideo, I hurriedly put the camera back in the front bicycle bag, where I also stored my day-to-day diary, and pedaled off to catch up with Jeff and Peter. I glanced down at the bag in about a mile or so and saw that it was open and that the camera and diary were gone. I back-tracked at least twice, examining every inch of the road and roadside. I then walked back along the route. No camera. No diary. They were gone. And I was in shock.

In that expensive camera were some 30 or more undeveloped photos, but far more important than the loss of the camera and photos, was the loss of the diary. It contained a record of each day's activity for the two months from November 11 to January 13—from our entrance into Nepal to about the time of Jeff's accident in Australia!

This was a major, major loss! I had every intention of writing a book after the World Ride was completed, and I had kept a most careful account of our wanderings for exactly that purpose. I was miserable beyond words—but I must say that Peter managed to cheer me up a bit by telling me that the author of *Lawrence of Arabia* had lost his entire manuscript at one point and had to go off by himself for four months to write another one. If he could manage it, I thought, I supposed that I could, too.

Anyway, the diary and camera were gone, and that was that, and I struggled with anger and frustration for quite some time afterward. For the next several days, Peter and Jeff generously helped me recall the more significant events of the two months recorded in the lost diary, and we were able to reconstruct them with surprising precision. Talk about teamwork! We may have missed a few items, but I'm very confident we didn't miss many.

Cheap Camping on the Coast

Rural Uruguay was a strange mixture of poverty and affluence. In one place we'd encounter an extremely up-scale town, with yachts in the harbor, but just down the road there were seedy restaurants, roads in miserable condition and the unmistakable evidence of widespread poverty. Nothing seemed to blend in logically from one place to another, but instead seemed to appear abruptly—completely different from one mile to the next. It made for interesting riding.

Campgrounds were everywhere. The largest one I've ever been in was north of La Paloma, where we found a National Park campground with 2,000 sites—and I'm sure nearly every site was occupied. This was vacation season, and there were just swarms of people in the park.

Sanitation was terrible, garbage and trash were everywhere, noise was incredible, and a cholera warning was posted in the showers. But it was cheap, $2.50 each, and the campsite was just where we wanted it, right on our route at the end of the day, so we settled in as best we could. Peter had to give up his Canadian passport before they'd let him in. Jeff and I were allowed to keep our American passports, and we all had to wear a security bracelet.

The campground was on the coast—an absolutely beautiful location. The following morning I went to the beach and spent some time on an outcropping of rocks—a pier of sorts—and watched some fishermen casting for sport (or lunch). Watching these fishermen cast, then reel in, then cast again and reel in, time after time, I was struck by the patience it took and how accurately it reflected our cancer fund-raising activities and our efforts to reach out again and again and bring something in. It would take the patience of these fishermen to achieve our goals, and I left the beach energized and rejuvenated with these thoughts in my mind.

Braving Brazil and the Banditos

As we neared the Brazilian border, we were focused on the horror stories we'd recently been told about traveling in that country. Reliable sources reported that banditos were everywhere waiting with machine-guns for tourists, stealing their cars, and maybe, in some cases, their lives. We heard it, unofficially, from diplomats in Montevideo and we heard it from a doctor who told us he'd "only been robbed once" on a visit to Brazil (not much encouragement there).

Other responsible people told us they wouldn't drive in Brazil after dark, or they'd drive at 110 miles an hour with their doors locked. We'd even gotten the message in Argentina. We were concerned—three guys on bikes would be a ripe target. The whole thing reminded me of the Finns telling us about the Russians. On the other hand, we met a couple who had just biked down through the southern portion of Brazil without a hint of a problem. They enjoyed every minute of it.

So, of course, we decided to get on with the biking, crossing over into Brazil on February 22.

Our itinerary called for five days of cycling in southern Brazil before catching a bus for the 1200-mile ride to Rio de Janeiro. People along our bike route couldn't have been friendlier. Motorists honked and waved at us, smiling and shouting, as if we were a visiting soccer team (big, big stuff in that part of the world). But each evening, as it became darker and the traffic built up, I had memories of some of the near-fatal roads in India.

10,054.2 Miles

Our first night in Brazil was spent in our tents behind a grocery store. We were soaked by rain and pummeled by wind, and we agreed that it was one of the worst nights of the trip. Two days later, heading for Pelotas where we were to board our bus for Rio, my brakes failed on one of the dirtiest and most trash-ridden roads I'd ever seen. With night coming on, this little highway was jammed with

speeding traffic and I ended up coasting into Pelotas, a little town that looked as if it had been built in 1940 and
never cleaned since.

We stayed in a motel for $10 each, including breakfast—
and it was here that we toasted our presence in the 32nd
country of the World Ride. We'd ridden 10,054.2 miles at
this precise point (compliments of Jeff's odometer and his
expert mileage record-keeping throughout the entire year-
long mission), and despite the surroundings, we went to
bed in good spirits.

In fact, the next morning, in preparation for my return to
the U.S. in a few days, I got a haircut and a beard trim. I
looked elegant.

In Pelotas, I also had my brakes repaired. I found a little
bike shop where the owner spoke English and he couldn't
have been nicer or more competent. Our experience in
Brazil, in short, was the opposite of what we had been led
to believe. I don't recall any instance where we weren't
treated in a friendly manner. No sign of banditos any-
where—although I don't discount the stories. I'm sure
they're out there, we just didn't run into them. I dropped a
$5 bill at the bus terminal in Pelotas and it was found by a
woman and returned to me. That's what I remember about
the people in Brazil.

Home Again, Home Again

It was a 30-hour bus trip to Rio. We took the bus from
Pelotas rather than further up the line because I absolutely

had to have 10 days or so in the U.S. before starting out on the U.S. tour and this was the only way to do it—to bike through Uruguay and a part of Brazil and then head to the U.S. This way, I could fulfill both commitments—completing the World Ride as promised and still allowing time to organize and coordinate the U.S. route for a strong finish to our round-the-world crusade.

Our stay in Rio was a one-night stand at a hotel on the beach—a hotel suggested to us by one of the customer representatives at the airline. It cost us $22 each—a terrific bargain—and how we would have liked to have spent some time in that fabulous city!

The next day, we flew north to Los Angeles and home to the U.S.A.!

Nineteen

THIS INCREDIBLE UNITED STATES!

California–Texas:
March 2–April 3

This is an amazing way of life we have—beyond the comprehension of most people in the world. On the long plane ride to Los Angeles, I understood what it must be like to come to America from such places as India or Estonia, or even from North Africa or some of the villages I'd seen in South America. It must really seem like a paradise of plenty.

In half the countries we visited, bread—the most basic of staples—was available in one form, sometimes two. Here, on the other hand, a third-world visitor would be bewildered by the seemingly infinite variety—white, rye, whole wheat, pumpernickel, mixed flours, sourdough, French, raisin, cinnamon, light, heavy, etc. There are muffins, rolls, doughnuts, bagels and on and on—different sizes, colors, quantities of everything. In the milk aisle they'd see whole milk, 2 percent fat, 1 percent fat or skim milk, not to mention chocolate milk, strawberry milk, buttermilk, cream and non-dairy creamers— powdered or evaporated milk.

Millions of people haven't even dreamed of such luxuries—or such incredible quantities of food. I once heard someone say that being wealthy means you can chose what you eat every day—something most people in the world will never experience.

The most noticeable thing about stores in third-world is how barren they are—nearly empty shelves, a few cans or boxes huddled together here and there, no refrigerated products. The focus is on survival—absolute minimum necessities to keep the body alive.

Mixed Emotions

Coming home, I knew what I was returning to and I felt grateful. Gone were the language barriers, the currency exchanges, the need for passports and visas. Gone were the gun-toting border guards and concerns about impromptu revolutions, polluted drinking water, insect-infested rooms, gravel-pit roads, suspicious authorities and the constant awareness of traveling through countries in which our bikes were worth a few year's wages to the people we passed.

No longer would I be worried about medical facilities or finding a bike shop or a place to eat. No more waiting in long lines to make a telephone call from a central office and no more insane costs for such calls. Here, I could drink the water, I could eat what I wanted as well as what I needed. Availability and cost were predictable, communications were sure, friends and Jaycees were immediately within reach. The sense of security found in traveling in one's own country was overwhelming.

But it was also less adventurous, and that was the downside. It was too predictable and too comfortable. After 31 foreign countries, coping with and experiencing the unexpected gets into your blood. You go to sleep at night with other cultures, other roads and other sights in your mind; odd memories jump out at you—haunting ones, compelling ones. A restlessness begins to creep in—a vague uneasiness—a desire to go back or keep going forward ... anything but stay where you are. On the flight to Los Angeles, I couldn't imagine taking off my biking gear and settling down—getting into a staid routine and doing what everybody else does. I'd become melded with my bike, couldn't see myself just parking it on the porch.

But we'd done what we'd set out to do—all but the last U.S. legs. There was a cause behind it all, and the further I flew toward the U.S., the more I focused on the U.S. route instead of the routes behind us. I was coming down from an adventurer's high—I knew that—much like a soldier returning from foreign duty or a ship captain from the sea. The reality of the present and the job that lie ahead asserted itself more and more as we neared Los Angeles.

The World Ride had left Boston with little more than great hopes. Now we had a track-record—people all over this planet had responded to our cancer crusade and supported it. The media had become aware of us, and now, with a last sprint across the U.S., we were in a position to capitalize on what we'd accomplished and raise significant amounts of money for cancer awareness and research.

Landing in Los Angeles

Ed Morales of the Pasadena Jaycees met us at the L.A. airport and we spent the next week working on administrative details. There was a lot to be done and the American Automobile Association generously offered to pick up phone and fax costs involved in coordinating the California-to-Boston route. Dave Juvet, Director of Public and Government Relations for the AAA Massachusetts/New Hampshire Division, had also outdone himself by alerting AAA offices along our U.S. route and requesting their support for the World Ride. (Many years earlier, I'd worked for AAA in Texas and I felt as if I were back at work with them again.)

Terry Senko, of the Pasadena Jaycees, housed me for the week and Jeff and Peter took the week off for R&R in Tucson. At a general Jaycee meeting in Pasadena, I met up again with Jane Brummelkamp (I'd seen her in Hong Kong). She had set up a companion ride bikathon around the Rose Bowl for the World Ride's benefit.

Upon my arrival I called Nancy, who thought she might be able to meet up with me in New Mexico for her birthday on April 1. What an enormous pleasure it was to pick up a phone and call her without endless delays and language problems. I also made dozens of administrative calls—cross-country strategy updates to the Jaycees, World Ride Project Managers and various sponsors. Steve Farrington, the JCI Senator in Vermont, said that the

Vermont JCI Senators had raised about $5,000 for the cancer crusade.

I reached about 85 percent of the people on my list. It was a week of good, solid, productive work—often putting in 12-hour days.

Jeff and Peter returned after their Tucson respite and we were off on our first leg of the U.S. route on March 13—everything was in order. Even if we'd come back from South America a few weeks earlier, I don't think things could have been better organized. We had high expectations of finishing our cancer awareness mission and fundraising efforts with a bang.

Across The Desert

Our route took us east from Pasadena through Pomona and Riverside and then on to Palm Springs. Beginning in Pasadena, and continuing throughout our U.S. route, several McDonald's Restaurant managers fed us free of charge—which helped our budgets considerably.

Connie Holt, a Palm Springs Jaycee, arranged for the team to be interviewed by the local NBC and ABC television affiliates. On the morning of one of the interviews our bikes were in a bike shop, so Connie drove over to get them and brought them back so we could be properly filmed by the TV crew.

We headed on to Twenty-nine Palms the next day, and then made a 119-mile run to Parker, Arizona—our bikes fully loaded. This was desert country—brutally hot and physically demanding. When it was over we opted for a comfortable motel where we could wash up at leisure and stretch out in a bed. The owner of the motel was from India. We fascinated him with some of our World Ride adventures in India, and he donated our room for the night. We ate dinner at a Pizza Hut, where we were again fed free of charge. There must be something about the desert air that brings out the generosity in people.

In retrospect, the three of us agreed that the four days of cycling from Palm Springs to Phoenix were among the most grueling of the World Ride. Atrocious heat, head winds, full bicycle loads, dust beyond belief, long miles between towns, and no shady rest areas certainly wasn't fun. We went through one small town in Arizona called Hope. Just on the other side of the town was a sign that read: NOW YOU'RE BEYOND HOPE.

We set up camp for the night about 10 miles past Hope, where we witnessed a glorious sunset followed by an incredibly brilliant moon and stars. The night sky was untouched by smog or humidity, and in the distance we could hear coyotes howling.

In The Limelight

In Phoenix we were hosted by Jeff's friends, Tony and Jan. It was Jan's mother whose battle against cancer had so affected Jeff, contributing to his motivation for making the World Ride. Mr. and Mrs. Ebert, Jeff's parents, had come in from Delaware and we all took a day off and relaxed. We also had a great newspaper interview in Phoenix, where as many as per-haps 50 photos were taken from every conceivable angle.

Vanessa Galvanek, the then Massachusetts Jaycee President, flew out to meet us in Phoenix. The Chrysler Corporation donated the use of a Plymouth Neon as a support vehicle from Phoenix to Boston. Vanessa drove the car for us from Phoenix to Albuquerque, N.M. Nancy was to meet us in Albuquerque where she would take over the driving as far as Lubbock, Texas. In Lubbock, Gary J.H. Wong, a Honolulu Jaycee, would take the wheel and drive all the way into Boston. Everything was carried out as planned.

We rode south from Phoenix to Tucson, where Jeff arranged for a one-hour team interview with the local NBC-TV affiliate. It went out on the NBC southwest feed and was picked up by many stations in several states. In all, things got off on good footing on our U.S. route. The only sour note was when 150 World Ride T-shirts that Nancy had shipped were lost by the carrier. Vanessa spent the bet-ter part of a day trying to find them, but she was told it would take a couple of weeks or more—maybe as many as six—to find and retrieve them. We were depending on the T-shirts to raise funds for the mission. We didn't know it then, but we were headed for another disappointment.

Overcome By Mountains

Starting out on the desert floor in Tucson, we ascend-ed to nearly 10,000 feet over the next few days. Peter was acclimated to the thin air of high altitudes, but Jeff and I weren't. Winded and tired, I started feeling the effects of the elevation as we pedaled along the high plateaus. Jeff's fatigue was complicated by what we later learned was a severe sinus infection. It was so cold in the mountains near the New Mexico border that my water bottles had frozen solid and my hands were numb. At one point we were in a near blizzard. Jeff was so ill that he couldn't go any further; he had to get in the Neon with Vanessa. Miraculously, he rode another leg two days later, but it aggravated his condition to the point where he was totally laid out until we were well into Texas. He was a lot sicker than he or anyone else knew.

My biggest handicap was the thin air and feeling winded constantly. Athletes often train in high altitudes so they can improve their wind and their competitive abilities. While I had heard this, I didn't quite understand it until that ride over the mountains from Arizona to New Mexico. I was in prime physical shape and had never faced breathing problems before.

Vanessa and I drove to Albuquerque where Vanessa left the team and where I picked Nancy up at the airport. I took the next day off and I justified it by arranging an interview with the Albuquerque NBC-TV station (they also agreed to pick up the Tucson southwest TV footage and air it). Following the interview, I met with the Albuquerque AAA folks and thanked them for support along our route.

Running Out of Steam in New Mexico

With Nancy back in the support vehicle it was just like old times—with Jeff in the car with her, as he'd been in New Zealand. We crossed southern New Mexico, which was expansive, flecked with high plateaus, and extremely desolate. One town we passed through had a total of two people in it. Food was a problem since there was no place to buy it. Nancy and Jeff were always scooting off ahead of us to round up something to eat. At one point, I remember actually shaking from hunger. Jeff was still quite ill, and my glands began to swell. Roswell was just ahead of us, however, a good-sized city, and Jeff and I visited a doctor. We were both given prescriptions for antibiotics, which seemed to do the trick. The doctor took a keen interest in our anti-cancer crusade and didn't charge us for the visits.

On the way to Tatum the next day, Nancy borrowed Jeff's bicycle to ride with me and Peter for 20 or 30 miles in the midst of strong tail winds. It was a real treat to have her beside me as a riding member of the World Ride team.

The tail wind continued long after Nancy had returned to the car, literally blowing us into west Texas—at one point enabling us to ride 60 miles in two-and-a-half hours! But the wind changed when we turned north to Lubbock and now came at us from the side. It took three hours to cover the last 30 miles into Lubbock—with west Texas soil clinging to every inch of our bodies, including our teeth.

Twenty

HELPING HANDS ACROSS AMERICA

Texas–Virginia:
April 3–May 11

Gary Wong, our new support-vehicle driver, met us at the Lubbock Airport April 3. He came all the way from Honolulu—eager to help, energetic and high-spirited. His coming, however, meant Nancy's going, but the World Ride was already a-third of the way along its U.S route. When Nancy and I said our goodbyes in Lubbock, we knew we were coming close to the end of these partings.

The team's next legs angled easterly through Ralls, Guthrie and Seymour, Texas—lonely and barren country. Now Peter started coming down with something and said he needed to see a doctor—and we took him to one as soon as we reached Wichita Falls. He was diagnosed with the same sinus infection that Jeff had and was prescribed antibiotics. I suppose that's what I had, too, but mine was less severe. Peter took only one day off, which we turned into a rest day for everyone. Jeff had been obliterated by the bug, but he was recovering well and was back on his bike when we left Wichita Falls.

Pam, our Jaycee host there, had arranged a room for us at no charge and treated us to dinner. We met with the Jaycees that evening, and the local CBS-TV station interviewed us at the meeting. At 11 the next morning, the local ABC-TV station also interviewed us.

Where, Oh Where, Is Our Driver?

We lost Gary on the leg to Duncan, Okla., about 65 miles north of Wichita Falls. It was the first time he drove solo (Jeff was back on his bike), and I guess we hadn't communicated our route clearly enough to him. I immediately began blaming myself for not being more specific with directions. Poor Gary—straight from Honolulu and driving around Texas and Oklahoma without a clue as to where he was or where he was going! At the same time we stopped at a gas station to call the sheriff for help, we spotted Gary driving past us down the road.

One of the guys at the gas station jumped in his truck and said, "Come on, mister, let's go get your buddy!" I got in and he drove at least 90 miles an hour until we caught up with him. I had to roll down the window and wave my arms wildly to get his attention and signal to him to turn around.

We met up with a dog on that leg of the trip who kept us company longer than any other dog had in all our world travels—he stayed with us for at least a mile, his tongue coming further and further out of his mouth, nearly touching his knees. I was tempted to stop and pat him or something or at least give him some water. Just as I was about to put my brakes on, he gave it up and started dragging himself back to wherever he came from. He was just a country mutt, but if I had to enter a dog in an endurance contest, I'd put him up against anything the American Kennel Club could offer.

Kid Talk

Rick Bickford of the American Automobile Association met us in Duncan and he had arranged for me to give a presentation at a National Geographic Society geography bee in nearby Oklahoma City. It was the statewide championships—big stuff—so I left the team and drove with Rick to the event. He had arranged a room for me, and the next morning I stood before a couple of hundred kids and parents and presented the World Ride story.

I gave a similar presentation to a couple of classes of students at an elementary school. The teachers brought the kids outside and I sat with them cross-legged on the grass and talked with them and displayed my bike and my paniers and my tool kit, answering their questions and generally having a great time.

Putting Wheels in Motion

While all this was going on, I made some calls and arranged a press conference for 6 p.m. on the steps of the capitol. NBC-TV showed up and so did my sister, who had been diagnosed as having pre-cancerous cells and whose threatening condition had contributed heavily to my founding the World Ride Against Cancer. She was accompanied by my nephew, J.W.

After the interview, we went to the hotel where the AAA had set me up the night before. They had arranged for two rooms for the second night in Oklahoma City—one for my sister and nephew and me and the other for the team.

Tulsa, Okla., about 100 miles north east of Oklahoma City, is the national headquarters of the U.S. Junior Chamber of Commerce. The team, my sister and nephew went to Tulsa to meet with the U.S. Jaycee staff. My sister and nephew had to leave after lunch, but it was heartwarming to have seen them, however briefly.

That evening, the team was welcomed by Matt Shapiro, the President of the U.S. Junior Chamber, and by his wife, Lisa, as well as by the Executive Vice President, Steve Lawson, and several others. Again we were treated to dinner and hotel accommodations. The following day, Chris Beach gave us a tour of the headquarters and we were the principal dignitaries at a raffle drawing the U.S. Junior Chamber staff had put together to raise funds for cancer research in honor of the World Ride—Jeff pulled out the tickets and Peter read off the numbers.

After the raffle, we were asked to sign a World Ride poster that was to be permanently displayed in the U.S. Junior Chamber of Commerce headquarters building—we felt honored.

Nearing The Southern States

We spent our last night in Oklahoma in Tahlequah, and headed out in the morning toward Fort Smith, Ark.

On April 15, tax day, we were just east of Little Rock, but since I hadn't earned a cent in the past two-and-a-half years, I just blew a kiss to a post office we passed along the way.

When we reached the Mississippi River, we had to put our bikes on the support vehicle before we could cross over to Memphis, Tenn. It was illegal to bike across the bridge—a restriction we encountered several times during the World Ride. The thing I remember most about our brief stay in Memphis was Gary's craving for Chinese food. We toured Memphis looking for a Chinese restaurant, and finally spotted one and Gary had to settle for some stir-fried chicken that was about as far removed from the real stuff as Memphis was from Peking.

It took four days to ride through Tennessee—from Memphis to Chattanooga—averaging about 80 miles a day. In Winchester, about 55 miles from Chattanooga, we were resting in the town square when a man walked up and offered to interview us for a local cable-TV show. It turned out that the man, whose name was Dale, was the anchorman for the show. As he interviewed us, he became more and more impressed with the World Ride mission, and offered to display the address of the World Ride organization for viewers interested in sending contributions toward cancer research.

I was especially looking forward to our Chattanooga stop because our original support-vehicle driver from Boston to Montreal, Jim Calder, had decided to drive down to meet up with us and catch up on things.

More Press

Jim Holloway, a JCI Senator, interviewed us for an NBC-TV show he regularly hosted in Chattanooga. The half-hour interview gave us the opportunity to tell the whole story of the World Ride. I was also able to meet briefly with Joe Eller, President of the U.S. JCI Senate. He had come to see us in Chattanooga and I was particularly anxious to show him that his confidence in our mission had not been misplaced.

Leaving Tennessee, we picked up the magnificent Blue Ridge Parkway a little north of Sylva, N.C. It was a steady 6,000-foot climb on the way to Asheville—tough riding. As night came on, we left the Parkway and rode into the suburbs to find a motel. When we found one, we also found one of the most amazing and uplifting persons we'd encountered on the entire World Ride.

Her name was Eloise and she was manager of the motel. She was a cancer survivor, and during her eight months of chemotherapy she had never missed a single day of work—and she worked six days a week!

I asked her how she could possibly accomplish such a feat, and she said it all had to do with her attitude. She had taken an irreversibly positive attitude toward her situation and she continued to work through the pain to maintain normalcy in her life. She said it was through her positive attitude and outlook that she managed to overcome the side-effects of the chemotherapy—it was an amazing example of courage and determination.

About 30 miles above Asheville, our route through North Carolina took us through Marion, Morganton, Spencer, Lexington, Greensboro and then on to Danville, Va. Television, newspaper and radio publicity in North Carolina was excellent, particularly in Morganton and Greensboro, where it seemed the media couldn't get enough of us—in some cases filming us as we left town. In Greensboro, I got a big hug from a woman who had a number of family members die of cancer—-much as in my own case—and I was deeply moved.

From the very first days of the World Ride, we encountered an astounding number of people whose lives had been affected by cancer. They'd go out of their way to express their support for our mission, and it was this—more than anything else—that kept the World Ride on track.

Back in Traffic

As we neared the Virginia border traffic increased considerably, an omen of the days ahead when we'd be biking the Washington/New York/Boston corridor. In fact, it got so bad at one point that trucks and cars began honking at us to get off the highway—which was a particularly dangerous one with narrow shoulders and no place to hide when the semis came too close. A State Trooper eventually pulled up behind us with his lights flashing and escorted us off the highway, giving us directions to a less heavily traveled parallel road. Unlike the excited cops in Italy who had fingered their guns when ordering us off the road, the

Trooper couldn't have been more pleasant and helpful.

In Danville, we were invited to meet with students at an elementary school. After giving us a standing ovation, we talked a bit about the World Ride and opened things up to questions and they had hundreds of them. The local ABC-TV station covered the meeting and even filmed us biking back to the hotel.

We passed the 13,000-mile mark near Franklin, Va., and met some Franklin Jaycees waiting for us along the road in the rain. They took us under cover, arranged a newspaper interview for us, and then sent us on our way to Virginia Beach the next morning where Tom Portante of the Jaycees had arranged accommodations for us. Wally Timmons of the AAA was also in Virginia Beach and he took some notes and photos for the regional AAA publication to provide up-to-date information on the World Ride and its crusade against cancer.

Roadside Rendezvous

A friend of Jeff's, Mark, temporarily joined our team in Virginia Beach, making us a foursome. As we were riding toward Williamsburg the next morning, I heard a woman screaming at me from a roadside restaurant—"Richa-a-a-ard! Richa-a-a-ard!" You guessed right—it was Nancy. I had expected to meet her in Williamsburg, where the Jaycees had arranged accommodations for all of us, including Nancy. But the roadside rendezvous was totally unexpected and we ran toward each other and hugged right in the middle of the road. She was waiting at the restaurant to board a train for Williamsburg and just happened to spot us cruising along.

I met up with her a few hours later in Williamsburg. She stayed for two days, taking in the sights of this restored colonial city while I attended to publicity matters. Her visit served to remind me how much I missed her and how much I wanted to complete our mission and rejoin friends and family—not to mention a normal life.

Family Matters

My family, in fact, was beginning to come very much into the picture as we entered the mid-Atlantic states and edged ever closer to New England. My uncle Richard, after whom I was named, lived in Waynesboro, Va., and I called him and asked if he and my aunt Ruth could meet me in Fredericksburg, where I'd be in two days. They could and they did—it was a loving reunion.

Our World Ride route enabled me to stay with my sister Betsey in Queens, N.Y., and also to see my uncle Wells—also in New York City—who told me my father would have been proud of the World Ride. On our route to Boston, we were to bike through Rye, N.Y., which was my childhood home and where I would visit my father's grave.

In the final legs of our journey, Jeff's family was to come into the picture as well. His parents lived in Newark, Del., and they kindly put us up while on our way to Philadelphia. This made the fourth time we'd seen Jeff's parents on the World Ride—they had become part of the World Ride's personal family. Jeff also had a brother and sister-in-law, Jim and Lorraine, in Glen Burnie, Md., and they, too, generously took us in for a night.

While we were not able to meet with President Clinton and Vice President Gore when we were in the Washington area, I was able to set up an interview with *USA Today* while in Arlington, Va.—a project I'd been working on for a year-and-a-half. Barbara Geehan, a reporter at the multi-million-circulation newspaper, had waited out the duration of the World Ride to receive a full account of our journey. She even arranged for us to have our picture taken near the famous statue of World War II's most famous photograph—the marines raising the American flag on a hilltop on Iwo Jima.

Twenty One

COMING HOME!

Virginia–Boston: May 11–May 28

I remained in the Arlington/Washington area for another day and managed to get several more interviews. On May 13, we biked from Glen Burnie, Md., to Rehoboth Beach, Del.

The Delaware Jaycees were holding a convention in Rehoboth Beach, and I gave a brief World Ride presentation to the group and received a substantial check to add to our fund-raising account. Chuck, a Jaycee whose mother had recently died of cancer, was instrumental in arranging for the impromptu presentation. We sold a number of World Ride T-shirts at the convention, which helped our T-shirt sales reach the $1,000 mark. By the time the World Ride project was completed, our fund-raising for cancer research topped $35,000.

Leaving Rehoboth Beach, we had at last set out on a relatively straight course for home—cycling up through Dover and then Newark, Del., and then on through the Philadelphia area and up through New Jersey to New York. In Somerville, N.J., the Jaycees arranged a reception for us at the Bicycling Hall of Fame and announced that they'd donate $1,000 donation to the World Ride's crusade.

Tender Places

As I mentioned earlier, I stayed with my sister, Betsey, in Queens, N.Y., and arrived there May 19—the day before Jackie Kennedy Onassis died of cancer.

Riding through New Rochelle, Larchmont and Rye, N.Y.—places where I had grown up—I remembered that I had bought my first 10-speed bike at the age of 11 or 12 with money I'd earned on my newspaper route. On the way home from the bike store, I cradled the back wheel in my arms as my Dad drove home in our station wagon. Here was where the events that had shaped my life took place, and here was the home of the grave of my father, who had died of cancer—the implacable killer that had also taken my mother and grandmother and was threatening my sister. Events which, indeed, not only shaped my life, but had directly led to my organizing and accomplishing the World Ride Against Cancer.

And now the ride was nearly done.

Striking Back

Riding around the world was the way I had chosen to strike back—the mission I had set for myself. In fulfilling the mission, I felt both pride and concern. I was proud of accomplishing my goal of increasing cancer awareness throughout the world, but I couldn't escape the reality that cancer still persisted and would continue to destroy countless families, as it had destroyed mine.

I feared that I hadn't done enough—that the message our team had taken to the world was too small a battle in the universal war against the disease. As I cycled through the home of my youth, haunted by childhood memories and the lives that had been so untimely taken by this dreaded disease, I knew that the World Ride mission had to continue—not on bikes, but perhaps through this book and through speaking engagements wherever I might be welcomed. The mission was not to stop at the finish line in Boston—it couldn't stop there—but to begin there. My focus on the disease and my commitment to engage in an all out war against it was more solid and passionate at the finish line than it had been at the starting gate—the ride served to strengthen my pledge.

The Come Down

It took some doing to come down from the high of having biked nearly 14,000 miles through 32 countries. The tremendous teamwork and organization of the World Ride—which was contributed to by so many—was what made our accomplishment possible. Sometimes, as I relive the challenges we faced on the road, and acknowledge the miracle of our overcoming them, I shake my head in a sheer sense of wonderment.

The exhilaration stayed with me for a while—I couldn't just shut it out of my head. And so did the ride, itself. After I got home, I wore my biking pants for weeks. The World Ride had completely taken over my life, and I had formed habits that were difficult to break. When I thought of going somewhere, I automatically thought in terms of riding a bike. Even today, when I bike somewhere, I occasionally find myself subconsciously expecting to see a waving Jaycee on some distant corner. It was an incredible experience.

The Homecoming Celebration

As we headed for the Massachusetts border and home, the emotions I experienced were overwhelming. Returning to New England had been central to my thoughts on every one of those many thousands of miles— yet when I actually arrived, it seemed to be just another tiny spot on the world map.

Crossing into Massachusetts, the East Longmeadow Jaycees hosted a welcome party for us and I saw several people whom I'd contacted a year-and-a-half earlier in quest of votes to secure the Massachusetts Jaycee Founding Sponsorship. I felt privileged to appear before these Jaycees and confirm the successful outcome of their decision to help us. Mark Smith, our World Ride Project manager in East Longmeadow, and his wife, Elayne, presented a $865 check to our cancer fund on behalf of the East Longmeadow Jaycees and local businesses.

On the following day, Jeff, Peter and I spent some time going through an atlas in the local library to reconstruct our routing during the period recorded in the diary I'd lost in Uruguay.

Shrewbury was our next stop, where we were hosted overnight by Brad, a JCI Senator, and then we went on to Lexington where we were met by loyal Jim Calder, who took Jeff and our bikes aboard his van while Peter and I took the Neon with Gary to the Salem town square to attend a reception in the team's honor.

It was a wonderful welcome party, and many supporters, sponsors and friends had gone out of their way to attend, including Vanessa, who'd driven our Plymouth support vehicle from Phoenix to Albuquerque, and Susie, who'd arranged to get the Neon from the Chrysler Corporation. Susie's sister, Liz, and her little dog, Molly, who had survived cancer, also attended—even the Salem High School Band was there!

Following the reception was a spaghetti festival at a social hall in Salem. Present were my sister Betsey and several other relatives, and most all of the same people who had wished us well at the starting line the year before. There was even a representative from the Salem mayor's office who read a proclamation acknowledging the World Ride's accomplishments and designating May 27, 1994, as Jaycee's World Ride Against Cancer Day. The following morning, we drove back to Lexington Center to resume the tail end of our ride.

The Final Leg

Accompanied by about 25 cyclists—several of whom were friends I had ridden with in Pan-Massachusetts

Challenges—we set out on the final 15 miles to Boston. Paula Markiewicz coordinated this "homecoming" leg, including food and rest stops for all the riders. The day was beautiful—enveloped in clear, blue skies—everything we could have hoped for. We proceeded to Boston's Waterfront Park—the official ending point of the World Ride—where we were surrounded by a wildly enthusiastic crowd and filmed and photographed by the Boston media.

David Wilson, President of the Massachusetts Jaycees, was there; Mr. White and Mr. Backer of the Service Corps of Retired Executives were there; several sponsors were on hand; Rob, a 5-year lung-cancer survivor was there, giving moving words of credit to the Dana-Farber Cancer Institute for his survival.

A Message To The World

I gave a short speech, acknowledging many of the principals who I had not seen in so long and who had made the World Ride possible, including Mark Herlihy and Diane Barow (the World Ride Project Managers for the Massachusetts Jaycees), Mary Canigiani and all the Massachusetts Jaycees who went above and beyond the call of duty to support the World Ride project. After the acknowledgments (hoping I hadn't missed anyone), I closed with the following thoughts—that cancer knows no borders, it doesn't discriminate as to age, sex, race or religion; and that the Jaycees' World Ride Against Cancer was meant to inspire people worldwide to join the fight against this terrible killer. "If we work together," I said, "we can accomplish extraordinary things to help end cancer in our lifetime." That was the message of the World Ride. And it is the message of this book.

There was another person at the Waterfront Park that day—George Gabriel Ash's mother. I walked over and hugged her—a long moment of closeness and I knew that George was there with us. And I knew he understood that this wasn't the end of the World Ride cause—that it was just the beginning. And wherever it would lead me, he'd come along with me, too—just as he had for the last 14,000 miles.

The World Ride had been dedicated to George, as will all that follows. We—all of us—have to destroy the killer that destroyed George Gabriel Ash.

EPILOGUE

Following the World Ride, I was determined to keep the mission alive by motivating and inspiring others to accomplish their goals, however difficult those goals might seem. By using my World Ride experiences as an illustration of the extraordinary results that can be brought about by inspired teamwork, I knew I could inspire audiences to work together to accomplish miracles of performance and overcome whatever obstacles lie before them in their own particular challenges. Nothing—nothing—is impossible to a team of individuals motivated to work together to go the extra mile in pursuit of a common goal.

For that reason, I started my own company—Going The Extra Mile/Speaking And Consulting. It seemed an appropriate name, and I speak before corporations, colleges, high schools and non-profit organizations worldwide.

PUBLISHER'S NOTE

The Sony Corporation of North America donated a camcorder to the World Ride in order for Richard to document his bicycle journey around the world. A 90 minute VHS video is available to you starting December 1, 1995. It features highlights from the World Ride and fascinating scenes of cultures very different from our own. The video makes a great companion piece to this book and can be ordered through the publisher for **$19.95 each (+ SH)**. To order please call or write:

MasterMedia Limited **1-800-334-8232** (M-F 8am-5pm)
c/o Haddon Craftsmen (717) 348-2193
1205 O'Neill Highway (717) 348-9247
Dunmore, PA 18512 *Visa and Mastercard Accepted*

BOOK TOUR SPONSORS

The A•D•S Group

AkPharma, Inc.

HIGHROAD

PRIME Development, Inc.

Share Group, Inc.

Vetta Sports, Inc.

ABOUT THE AUTHOR

Richard Drorbaugh, 33, graduated from the University of Massachusetts and is a businessman with experience in sales and marketing, public relations and nonprofit management. He was chosen as one of 1995's Ten Outstanding Young Leaders by the Boston Jaycees.

Drorbaugh, a member of the National Speakers Association that represents America's youth at its best, is in demand on college campuses, for nonprofit and corporate audiences who want to hear about his ride and personal triumph over tragedy.

The World Ride Team was featured in USA Today, The Boston Globe and on television and radio worldwide.

Drorbaugh is available as a key-note speaker. Please contact MasterMedia's Speakers' Bureau for availability and fee arrangements. Call Tony Colao at 908-359-1612, or fax: 908-359-1647.

Other MasterMedia Books

To order MasterMedia books, either visit your local bookstore or call 800-334-8232.

AGING PARENTS AND YOU: A Complete Handbook to Help You Help Your Elders Maintain a Healthy, Productive and Independent Life, by Eugenia Anderson-Ellis, is a complete guide to providing care to aging relatives. It gives practical advice and resources to the adults who are helping their elders lead productive and independent lives. Revised and updated. ($9.95 paper)

BALANCING ACTS! Juggling Love, Work, Family and Recreation, by Susan Schiffer Stautberg and Marcia Worthing, provides strategies to achieve a balanced life by reordering priorities and setting realistic goals. ($12.95 paper)

BEATING THE AGE GAME: Redefining Retirement, by Jack and Phoebe Ballard, debunks the myth that retirement means sitting out the rest of the game. The years between 55 and 80 can be your best, says the authors, who provide ample examples of people successfully using retirement to reinvent their lives. ($12.95 paper)

THE BIG APPLE BUSINESS AND PLEASURE GUIDE: 501 Ways to Work Smarter, Play Harder, and Live Better in New York City, by Muriel Siebert and Susan Kleinman, offers visitors and New Yorkers alike advice on how to do business in the city and enjoy its attractions. ($9.95 paper)

BREATHING SPACE: Living and Working at a Comfortable Pace in a Sped-Up Society, by Jeff Davidson, helps readers to handle information and activity overload and gain greater control over their lives. ($10.95 paper)

CARVING WOOD AND STONE, by Arnold Prince, is an illustrated step-by-step handbook demonstrating all you need to hone your wood and carving skills. ($15.95 paper)

THE COLLEGE COOKBOOK II, For Students by Students, by Nancy Levicki, is a handy volume of recipes culled from college students across the country. ($11.95 paper)

THE CONFIDENCE FACTOR: How Self-Esteem Can Change Your Life, by Dr. Judith Briles, is based on a nationwide survey of 6,000 men and women. Briles explores why women often feel a lack of self-confidence and have a poor opinion of themselves. She offers step-by-step advice on becoming the person you want to be. ($12.95 paper, $18.95 cloth)

CUPID, COUPLES & CONTRACTS: A Guide to Living Together, Prenuptial Agreements, and Divorce, by Lester Wallman, with Sharon McDonnell, is an insightful, consumer-oriented handbook that provides a comprehensive overview of family law, including prenuptial agreements, alimony and fathers' rights. ($12.95 paper)

THE DOLLARS AND SENSE OF DIVORCE: The Financial Guide for Women, by Dr. Judith Briles, is the first book to combine the legal hurdles by planning finances before, during and after divorce. ($10.95 paper)

FINANCIAL SAVVY FOR WOMEN: A Money Book for Women of All Ages, by Dr. Judith Briles, divides a woman's monetary lifespan into six phases, discusses specific issues to be addressed at each stage and demonstrates how to create a sound money plan. ($15.00 paper)

FLIGHT PLAN FOR LIVING: The Art of Self-Encouragement, by Patrick O'Dooley, is a guide organized like a pilot's checklist, to ensure you'll be flying "clear to the top" throughout your life. ($17.95 cloth)

HERITAGE: The Making of the American Family, by Robert Pamplin Jr., Gary Eisler, Jeff Sengstack, and John Domini, mixes history and philosophy in a biographical saga of the Pamplins' phenomenal ascent to wealth and the creation of one of the largest private fortunes in the U.S. ($24.95 cloth)

HOT HEALTH-CARE CAREERS, by Margaret McNally and Phyllis Schneider, offers readers what they need to know about training for and getting jobs in a rewarding field where professionals are always in demand. ($10.95 paper)

LIFETIME EMPLOYABILITY: How to Become Indispensible, by Carole Hyatt, shows readers how to take a fresh look at their career paths, adapt to the current marketplace by using old skills in new way and discover options they didn't know they had. ($12.95 paper)

HOW TO GET WHAT YOU WANT FROM ALMOST ANYBODY, by T. Scott Gross, shows how to get great service, negotiate better prices and always get what you pay for. ($9.95 paper)

KIDS WHO MAKE A DIFFERENCE, by Joyce Roché and Marie Rodriguez, is an inspiring document on how today's toughest challenges are being met by teenagers and kids, whose courage and creativity enables them to find practical solutions! ($8.95 paper, with photos)

LEADING YOUR POSITIVELY OUTRAGEOUS SERVICE TEAM, by T. Scott Gross, forgoes theory in favor of a hands-on approach, Gross providing a step-by-step formula for developing self-managing service teams that put the customer first. ($12.95 paper)

LIFE'S THIRD ACT: Taking Control of Your Mature Years, by Patricia Burnham, Ph.D., is a perceptive handbook for everyone who recognizes that planning is the key to enjoying your mature years. ($10.95 paper, $18.95 cloth)

LISTEN TO WIN: A Guide to Effective Listening, by Curt Bechler and Richard Weaver, Ph.D.s, is a powerful, people-oriented book that will help you learn to live with others, connect with them, get the best from them and empower them. ($18.95 cloth)

THE LIVING HEART BRAND NAME SHOPPER'S GUIDE, (3d edition), by Michael DeBakey, M.D., Antonio Gotto, Jr., M.D., Lynne Scott, M.A., R.D./L.D., and John Foreyt, Ph.D., lists brand name products low in fat, saturated fatty acids and cholesterol. (14.95 paper)

THE LIVING HEART GUIDE TO EATING OUT, by Michael DeBakey, Antonio Gotto, Jr., Lynne Scott, is an essential handbook for people who want to maintain a health-conscious diet when dining in all types of restaurants. ($9.95 paper)

MAKING YOUR DREAMS COME TRUE NOW!, by Marcia Wieder, introduces an easy, unique, and practical technique for defining, pursuing, and realizing your career and life interests. Filled with stories of real people and helpful exercises, plus a personal workbook. (Revised and updated, $10.95 paper)

MANAGING IT ALL: Time-Saving Ideas for Career, Family, Relationships, and Self, by Beverly Benz Treuille and Susan Schiffer Stautberg, is written for women who are juggling careers and families. More than 200 career women (ranging from a TV anchorwoman to an investment banker) were interviewed. The book contains many humorous anecdotes on saving time and improving the quality of life for self and family. ($9.95 paper)

MANAGING YOUR CHILD'S DIABETES, by Robert Wood Johnson IV, Sale Johnson, Casey Johnson, and Susan Kleinman, brings help to families trying to understand diabetes and control its effects. ($10.95 paper)

MANAGING YOUR PSORIASIS, by Nicholas J. Lowe, M.D., is an innovative manual that couples scientific research and encouraging support, with an emphasis on how patients can take charge of their health. ($10.95 paper, $17.95 cloth)

MANN FOR ALL SEASONS: Wit and Wisdom from The Wahington Post's Judy Mann, shows the columnist at her best as she writes about women, families and the impact and politics of the women's revolution. ($9.95 paper, $19.95 cloth)

MIND YOUR OWN BUSINESS: And Keep it in the Family, by Marcy Syms, CEO of Syms Corp., is an effective guide for any organization facing the toughest step in managing a family business—making the transition to the new generation. ($12.95 paper, $18.95 cloth)

OFFICE BIOLOGY: Why Tuesday is the Most Productive Day and Other Relevant Facts fro Survival in the Workplace, by Edith Weiner and Arnold Brown, teaches how in the '90s and beyond we will be expected to work smarter, take better control of our health, adapt to advancing technology and improve our lives in ways that are not too costly or resource-intensive. ($12.95 paper, $21.95 cloth)

ON TARGET: Enhance Your Life and Advance Your Career, by Jeri Sedlar and Rick Miners, is a neatly woven tapestry of insights on career and life issues gathered from audiences across the country. This feedback has been crystallized into a highly readable guide for exploring what you want. ($11.95 paper)

PAIN RELIEF: How to Say No to Acute, Chronic, and Cancer Pain!, by Dr. Jane Cowles, offers a step-by-step plan for assessing pain and communicating it to your doctor, and explains the importance of having a pain plan before undergoing any medical or surgical treatment. Includes "The Pain Patient's Bill of Rights," and a reusable pain assessment chart. ($14.95 paper, $22.95 cloth)

POSITIVELY OUTRAGEOUS SERVICE: New and Easy Ways to Win Customers for Life, by T. Scott Gross, identifies what '90s consumers really want and how business can develop effective marketing strategies to answer those needs. ($14.95 paper)

THE PREGNANCY AND MOTHERHOOD DIARY: Planning the First Year of Your Second Career, by Susan Schiffer Stautberg, is the first and only undated appointment diary that shows how to manage pregnancy and career. ($12.95 spiralbound)

REAL BEAUTY...REAL WOMEN: A Handbook for Making the Best of Your Own Good Looks, by Kathleen Walas, international beauty and fashion director of Avon Products, Inc., offers expert advice on beauty and fashion for women of all ages and ethnic backgrounds. ($19.50 paper)

ROSEY GRIER'S ALL-AMERICAN HEROES: Multicultural Success Stories, by Roosevelt "Rosey" Grier, is a candid collection of profiles of prominent African-Americans, Latins, Asians, and Native Americans who revealed how they achieved public acclaim and personal success. ($9.95 paper, with photos)

A SEAT AT THE TABLE: An Insider's Guide for America's New Women Leaders, by Patricia Harrison. A must-read guide that offers practical advice for women who want to serve on boards of directors, play key roles in politics and community affairs or become policy makers in public or private sectors.($19.95 cloth)

SELLING YOURSELF: Be the Competent, Confident Person You Really Are!, by Kathy Thebo, Joyce Newman, and Diana Lynn. The ability to express yourself effectively and to project a confident image is essential in today's fast-paced world where professional and personal lines frequently cross. ($12.95 paper)

SHOCKWAVES: The Global Impact of Sexual Harassment, by Susan L. Webb, examines the problem of sexual harassment today in every kind of workplace around the world. Practical and well-researched, this manual provides the most recent information available, including legal changes in progress. ($11.95 paper, $19.95 cloth)

SOMEONE ELSE'S SON, by Alan Winter, explores the parent-child bond in a contemporary novel of lost identities, family secrets and relationships gone awry. Eighteen years after bringing their first son home from the hospital, Tish and Brad Hunter discover they are not his biological parents. ($18.95 cloth)

STEP FORWARD: Sexual Harassment in the Workplace, by Susan L. Webb, presents the facts for dealing with sexual harassment on the job. ($9.95 paper)

THE STEPPARENT CHALLENGE: A Primer for Making it Work, by Stephen Williams, Ph.D., offers insight into the many aspects of step relationships—from financial issues to lifestyle changes to differences in race or religion that affect the whole family. ($13.95 paper)

STRAIGHT TALK ON WOMEN'S HEALTH: How to Get the Health Care You Deserve, by Janice Teal, Ph.D., and Phyllis Schneider, is destined to become a health-care "bible." Devoid of confusing medical jargon, it offers a wealth of resources, including contact lists of health lines and women's medical centers. ($14.95 paper)

TEAMBUILT: Making Teamwork Work, by Mark Sanborn, teaches businesses how to increase productivity, without increasing resources or expenses, by building teamwork among employees. ($12.95 paper, $19.95 cloth)

A TEEN'S GUIDE TO BUSINESS: The Secrets to a Successful Enterprise, by Linda Menzies, Oren Jenkins, and Rick Fisher, provides solid information about starting your own business or working for one ($7.95 paper)

WHAT KIDS LIKE TO DO, by Edward Stautberg, Gail Wubbenhorst, Atiya Easterling, and Phyllis Schneider, is a handy guide for parents, grandparents, and baby sitters. Written by kids for kind, this is an easy-to-read, generously illustrated primer for teaching families how to make every day more fun. ($7.95 paper)

WHEN THE WRONG THING IS RIGHT: How to Overcome Conventional Wisdom, Popular Opinion, and All the Lies Your Parents Told You, by Sylvia Bigelson, Ed.S., and Virginia McCullough, addresses issues such as marriage, relationships, parents and siblings, divorce, sex, money and careers, and encourages readers to break free from the pressures of common wisdom and to trust their own choices. ($9.95 paper)

WHY MEN MARRY: Insights From Marrying Men, by A.T. Langford, interviews with 64 men revealing their views on marriage. These men describe what scares them about women, how potential partners are tested, and how it feels to be a "marriage object." ($18.95 cloth)

A WOMAN'S PLACE IS EVERYWHERE: Inspirational Profiles of Female Leaders Who are Expanding the Roles of American Women, by Lindsey Johnson and Jackie Joyner-Kersee, profiles 30 women whose personal and professional achievements are helping to shape and expand our ideas of what's possible for humankind. ($9.95 paper)

THE WORKING MOM ON THE RUN MANUAL: A humorous practical guide for working parents, particularly single, working Moms. Offers insights about careers, disciplining the kids, coping with husbands who won't do housework, running a home-based business and keeping track of just about everything every day, by Debbie Nigro. ($9.95 paper)

YOUR VISION: All About Modern Eye Care, by Warren D. Cross Jr., M.D., and Lawrence Lynn, Ph.D., reveals astounding research discoveries in an entertaining and informative handbook written with the patient in mind. ($13.95 paper)